Teach Yourself
VISUALLY™
Laptops

Visual

by Nancy Muir

BICENTENNIAL
1807
WILEY
2007
BICENTENNIAL

Wiley Publishing, Inc.

Teach Yourself VISUALLY™ Laptops

Published by
Wiley Publishing, Inc.
111 River Street
Hoboken, NJ 07030-5774

Published simultaneously in Canada

Library of Congress Control Number: 2007936454

ISBN: 978-0-470-17111-0

Manufactured in the United States of America

10 9 8 7 6 5 4 3 2 1

Trademark Acknowledgments

Contact Us

For general information on our other products and services please contact our Customer Care Department within the U.S. at 800-762-2974, outside the U.S. at 317-572-3993 or fax 317-572-4002.

For technical support please visit www.wiley.com/techsupport.

WILEY

Wiley Publishing, Inc.

Sales

Contact Wiley
at (800) 762-2974 or
fax (317) 572-4002.

Praise for Visual Books

"Like a lot of other people, I understand things best when I see them visually. Your books really make learning easy and life more fun."

John T. Frey (Cadillac, MI)

"I have quite a few of your Visual books and have been very pleased with all of them. I love the way the lessons are presented!"

Mary Jane Newman (Yorba Linda, CA)

"I just purchased my third Visual book (my first two are dog-eared now!), and, once again, your product has surpassed my expectations.

Tracey Moore (Memphis, TN)

"I am an avid fan of your Visual books. If I need to learn anything, I just buy one of your books and learn the topic in no time. Wonders! I have even trained my friends to give me Visual books as gifts."

Illona Bergstrom (Aventura, FL)

"Thank you for making it so clear. I appreciate it. I will buy many more Visual books."

J.P. Sangdong (North York, Ontario, Canada)

"I have several books from the Visual series and have always found them to be valuable resources."

Stephen P. Miller (Ballston Spa, NY)

"Thank you for the wonderful books you produce. It wasn't until I was an adult that I discovered how I learn – visually. Nothing compares to Visual books. I love the simple layout. I can just grab a book and use it at my computer, lesson by lesson. And I understand the material! You really know the way I think and learn. Thanks so much!"

Stacey Han (Avondale, AZ)

"I absolutely admire your company's work. Your books are terrific. The format is perfect, especially for visual learners like me. Keep them coming!"

Frederick A. Taylor, Jr. (New Port Richey, FL)

"I have several of your Visual books and they are the best I have ever used."

Stanley Clark (Crawfordville, FL)

"I bought my first Teach Yourself VISUALLY book last month. Wow. Now I want to learn everything in this easy format!"

Tom Vial (New York, NY)

"Thank you, thank you, thank you...for making it so easy for me to break into this high-tech world. I now own four of your books. I recommend them to anyone who is a beginner like myself."

Gay O'Donnell (Calgary, Alberta, Canada)

"I write to extend my thanks and appreciation for your books. They are clear, easy to follow, and straight to the point. Keep up the good work! I bought several of your books and they are just right! No regrets! I will always buy your books because they are the best."

Seward Kollie (Dakar, Senegal)

"Compliments to the chef!! Your books are extraordinary! Or, simply put, extra-ordinary, meaning way above the rest! THANK YOU THANK YOU THANK YOU! I buy them for friends, family, and colleagues."

Christine J. Manfrin (Castle Rock, CO)

"What fantastic teaching books you have produced! Congratulations to you and your staff. You deserve the Nobel Prize in Education in the Software category. Thanks for helping me understand computers."

Bruno Tonon (Melbourne, Australia)

"Over time, I have bought a number of your 'Read Less - Learn More' books. For me, they are THE way to learn anything easily. I learn easiest using your method of teaching."

José A. Mazón (Cuba, NY)

"I am an avid purchaser and reader of the Visual series, and they are the greatest computer books I've seen. The Visual books are perfect for people like myself who enjoy the computer, but want to know how to use it more efficiently. Your books have definitely given me a greater understanding of my computer, and have taught me to use it more effectively. Thank you very much for the hard work, effort, and dedication that you put into this series."

Alex Diaz (Las Vegas, NV)

Credits

Project Editor
Tim Borek

Acquisitions Editor
Jody Lefevere

Copy Editor
Marylouise Wiack

Technical Editor
Alex Kingman

Editorial Manager
Robyn Siesky

Business Manager
Amy Knies

Sr. Marketing Manager
Sandy Smith

Manufacturing
Allan Conley
Linda Cook
Paul Gilchrist
Jennifer Guynn

Special Help
Alissa Birkel
Chris Wolfgang

Book Design
Kathie Rickard

Production Coordinator
Adrienne Martinez

Layout
Carrie A. Cesavice
Stephanie D. Jumper
Jennifer Mayberry
Amanda Spagnuolo

Screen Artist
Joyce Haughey
Jill Proll

Illustrators
Jonelle Burns
Ronda David-Burroughs
Cheryl Grubbs
Shane Johnson
Jake Mansfield

Proofreader
Broccoli Information
Management

Quality Control
Melanie Hoffman

Indexer
Broccoli Information
Management

**Vice President and Executive
Group Publisher**
Richard Swadley

Vice President and Publisher
Barry Pruett

Composition Director
Debbie Stailey

About the Author

Nancy Muir is the author of over 50 books on technology, business, and science topics. Nancy holds a certificate in Distance Learning Design, and has held management positions in both the software and publishing industries. Nancy has been an instructor in technical writing at a midwestern university and currently co-teaches a distance learning course on Internet Safety through Washington State University.

Author's Acknowledgments

The author wishes to thank Jody Lefevere for offering her the opportunity to write this book, and Tim Borek for his able sheparding of the project. Thanks also to Marylouise Wiack for her able copy editing, and Alex Kingman for his alert technical editing.

Table of Contents

chapter 3 Buying Your Laptop

chapter 4 Setting Up Your New Laptop

Table of Contents

chapter 7 File Management Basics

chapter 8 Software Basics

Table of Contents

chapter 9 Using Software

chapter 10 Connecting to a Network

chapter 11   **Exploring the Internet**

chapter 12   **Communicating Online**

Table of Contents

chapter 13 Managing Power

chapter 14 Maintaining Your Laptop

chapter 15 Computer Security

How To Use This Book

How to Use this Teach Yourself VISUALLY Book

Do you look at the pictures in a book or newspaper before anything else on a page? Would you rather see an image instead of read about how to do something? Search no further. This book is for you. Opening *Teach Yourself VISUALLY Laptops* allows you to read less and learn more about laptop and portable computers.

Who Needs This Book

This book is for a reader who has never used this particular technology or software application. It is also for more computer-literate individuals who want to expand their knowledge of the different features that laptops have to offer.

Book Organization

Teach Yourself VISUALLY Laptops has 15 chapters.

Chapter 1, "Introducing the Laptop," provides an overview of laptop computers and how they differ from a desktop, as well as examining the various slots, ports, and drives of a laptop.

Chapter 2, "Choosing Laptop Peripherals and Accessories," is a guide to the various input, storage, security, power, and sound devices you might use with a laptop.

Chapter 3, "Buying Your Laptop," explains what you should look for when buying your laptop computer.

Chapter 4, "Setting Up Your New Laptop," explores how you set up your computer when you take it out of the box and the basics of working with a mouse and keyboard.

Chapter 5, "Working with a Macintosh," provides an overview of the Macintosh operating system and how you work in the Macintosh environment.

Chapter 6, "Exploring Windows Vista," teaches you how to move around the Windows Vista desktop, work with system volume, the Recycle Bin, and Sidebar. You also learn how to find files with Windows Explorer, modify your screen's appearance, and get help.

Chapter 7, "File Management Basics," shows you how to work with files and folders to organize the data you work with on your computer, and save files to a CD, DVD, or flash drive.

Chapter 8, "Software Basics," covers everything from installing a program to uninstalling a program, how to open documents, use menus and toolbars, work with dialog boxes, and print documents.

Chapter 9, "Using Software," provides information about working in common software programs such as a word processor, spreadsheet, database, or presentation program.

Chapter 10, "Connecting to a Network," explains how to set up a wireless or wired connection that you can use to share files or online connections.

Chapter 11, "Exploring the Internet," demonstrates how to connect to the Internet, and perform a variety of activities online, such as searching, working with favorite sites, shop, research, or download files.

Chapter 12, "Communicating Online," introduces you to the ins and outs of e-mailing, instant messaging, and making phone calls via your computer and an Internet connection. In addition, this chapter covers blogs and social sites.

Chapter 13, "Managing Power," shows you how to get the most out of your battery power when you take your laptop on the road.

Chapter 14, "Maintaining Your Laptop," explains how to care for and protect your investment.

Chapter 15, "Computer Security," introduces you to the various tools and utilities that Windows Vista and Internet Explorer provide to keep your information safe while online.

Chapter Organization

This book consists of sections, all listed in the book's table of contents. A *section* is a set of steps that show you how to complete a specific computer task.

Each section, usually contained on two facing pages, has an introduction to the task at hand, a set of full-color screen shots and steps that walk you through the task, and a set of tips. This format allows you to quickly look at a topic of interest and learn it instantly.

Chapters group together three or more sections with a common theme. A chapter may also contain pages that give you the background information needed to understand the sections in a chapter.

What You Need to Use This Book

You need not have already purchased a laptop to begin using this book, as Chapters 1 and 2 contain information helpful in selecting your ideal laptop computer. If you already have access to a laptop, however, you can move on to the wealth of information about setting up and using your laptop in the rest of the chapters of this book.

Using the Mouse

This book uses the following conventions to describe the actions you perform when using the mouse:

Click

Press your left mouse button once. You generally click your mouse on something to select something on the screen.

Double-click

Press your left mouse button twice. Double-clicking something on the computer screen generally opens whatever item you have double-clicked.

Right-click

Press your right mouse button. When you right-click anything on the computer screen, the program displays a shortcut menu containing commands specific to the selected item.

Click and Drag, and Release the Mouse

Move your mouse pointer and hover it over an item on the screen. Press and hold down the left mouse button. Now, move the mouse to where you want to place the item and then release the button. You use this method to move an item from one area of the computer screen to another.

The Conventions in This Book

A number of typographic and layout styles have been used throughout *Teach Yourself VISUALLY Laptops* to distinguish different types of information.

Bold

Bold type represents the names of commands and options that you interact with. Bold type also indicates text and numbers that you must type into a dialog box or window.

Italics

Italic words introduce a new term and are followed by a definition.

Numbered Steps

You must perform the instructions in numbered steps in order to successfully complete a section and achieve the final results.

Bulleted Steps

These steps point out various optional features. You do not have to perform these steps; they simply give additional information about a feature.

Indented Text

Indented text tells you what the program does in response to you following a numbered step. For example, if you click a certain menu command, a dialog box may appear, or a window may open. Indented text may also tell you what the final result is when you follow a set of numbered steps.

Notes

Notes give additional information. They may describe special conditions that may occur during an operation. They may warn you of a situation that you want to avoid, for example the loss of data. A note may also cross reference a related area of the book. A cross reference may guide you to another chapter, or another section with the current chapter.

Icons and buttons

Icons and buttons are graphical representations within the text. They show you exactly what you need to click to perform a step.

 You can easily identify the tips in any section by looking for the TIPS icon. Tips offer additional information, including tips, hints, and tricks. You can use the TIPS information to go beyond what you have learn learned in the steps.

Operating System Difference

In many cases you can follow along with the steps in this book regardless of whether your computer is running the Mac OS or Windows operating system. Except for chapters specifically focused on Windows Vista (such as Chapter 6), we have included notes when the procedures on a Mac laptop differ somewhat.

Introducing the Laptop

Portable computers, referred to as notebooks or laptops, began as a great tool for people who travel and want to take their computer along. Today, laptops with high-end displays and huge processing power are taking over the desktop, as well.

Explore a Laptop

Although laptop models vary by weight, size, keyboard configuration, and more, they share some common traits in a compact package.

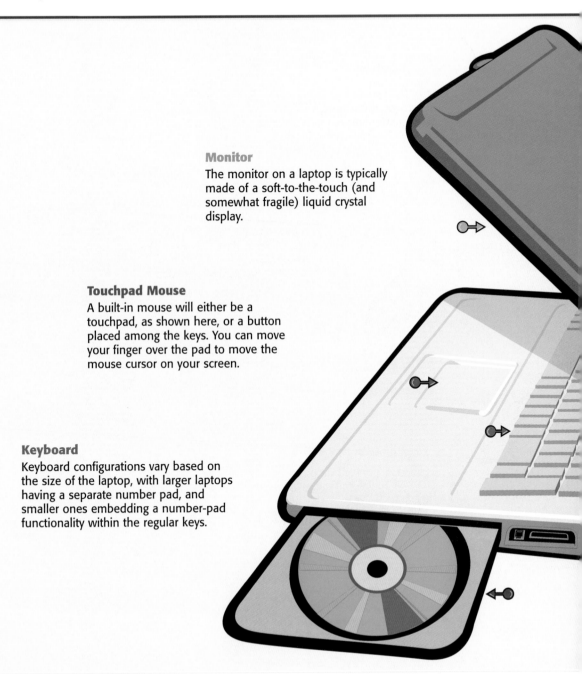

Monitor

The monitor on a laptop is typically made of a soft-to-the-touch (and somewhat fragile) liquid crystal display.

Touchpad Mouse

A built-in mouse will either be a touchpad, as shown here, or a button placed among the keys. You can move your finger over the pad to move the mouse cursor on your screen.

Keyboard

Keyboard configurations vary based on the size of the laptop, with larger laptops having a separate number pad, and smaller ones embedding a number-pad functionality within the regular keys.

Function Keys

Most laptops have
pre-assigned functions for these
aptly named function keys. Typical
uses are for muting the speakers
or accessing the Internet.

DVD Drive

Most newer laptops include
a DVD drive, although some still
use a CD drive. The location of
these drives varies by model.

Battery

A battery usually slots into the
bottom of a laptop and needs to
be recharged on a regular basis.

In many important ways, a laptop computer and desktop are the same. They are both used for the same functions: Both can be connected to devices such as printers; both contain a hard drive and operating system; and both run hardware and store files. However, there are some interesting differences.

Size

Laptops are built for portability, while the average desktop computer includes a large central processing unit (CPU) tower and monitor.

Input Devices

Laptops have a built-in keyboard and mouse. Desktops use a plug-in or wireless keyboard and mouse. However, you can also plug a standard keyboard or mouse into your laptop if you wish.

Monitor

If your desktop monitor wears out, you can replace it. This is not the case with a laptop, where the monitor is attached to the CPU.

Power Source

Laptops use a battery that is charged by plugging the laptop into an electrical outlet. Desktops only run through an electrical outlet.

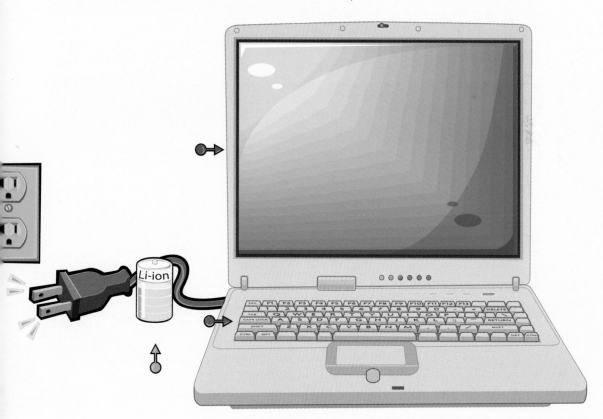

Different manufacturers build a wide variety of laptops with a large range of prices and features.

Macintosh

Current laptops from Apple are the MacBook (the lower-priced line) and the MacBook Pro. These laptops are only built for Apple, and have a unique operating system. Both the computers and operating system are only available from Apple through its Web site or through Apple reseller stores.

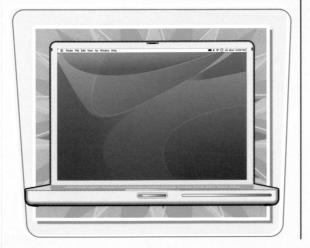

Windows-based PCs

Laptops with the Microsoft Windows operating system installed are referred to as PCs, which stands for personal computers. They are made by a variety of manufacturers. You can buy the Windows operating system separately.

Tablet PCs

Tablet PCs are Windows-based machines with a different hardware configuration. They come in a tablet configuration that is similar to a machine version of a legal pad, and a clamshell variety that looks more like a traditional laptop, but that converts into a tablet by swinging the monitor on hinges. You can input data by writing directly on Tablet PC screens using a stylus.

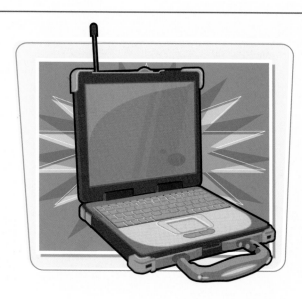

Rugged Laptops

Some laptops are marketed for the durability of their chassis. Useful for people who work in industries such as construction or archeology, these models are both more water- and shock-proof than their non-rugged counterparts. Their keyboards are sealed to prevent water damage, they can withstand more variation in temperature, and they can function near electromagnetic transmissions, such as from power generators, without being damaged.

continued

Ultra Portable

Some laptops are designed for travel, weighing in at between two and three pounds. They offer a smaller display and keyboard size, but have the advantage of a longer battery life.

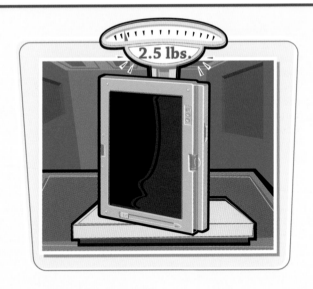

Desktop

Today laptops are taking over the desktop, with models that use 17- or even 20-inch monitors and full keyboards with number pads. With wireless Internet connections and a built-in keyboard and mouse, they tend to reduce the clutter of cables that come with standard desktop models.

Multimedia and Gaming

Laptops that can handle graphics and animations that appear in many computer games tend to have powerful graphics cards, large screens with high resolution, a lot of memory, and fast processors. These come with a high price tag, but for a dedicated gamer or multimedia designer, they may be worth it.

Handhelds

Some very small laptops, referred to as handhelds, are showing up in the market, such as the Sony Vaio UX Micro PC. This Windows Vista-based machine has a 4.5-inch screen, weighs 1.2 pounds, and can get up to 4.5 hours of battery life. If you do not need to type long documents on the tiny keyboard, the small size may work well in your travels.

The arrangement of various slots and ports around your laptop may vary, but most are on the sides or back of the chassis. Besides the power cord connector, you will find the following slots and ports on most laptops.

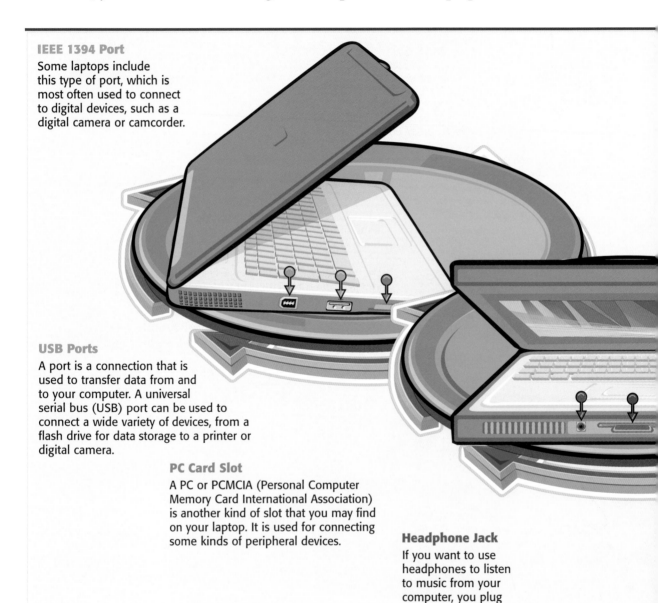

IEEE 1394 Port

Some laptops include this type of port, which is most often used to connect to digital devices, such as a digital camera or camcorder.

USB Ports

A port is a connection that is used to transfer data from and to your computer. A universal serial bus (USB) port can be used to connect a wide variety of devices, from a flash drive for data storage to a printer or digital camera.

PC Card Slot

A PC or PCMCIA (Personal Computer Memory Card International Association) is another kind of slot that you may find on your laptop. It is used for connecting some kinds of peripheral devices.

Headphone Jack

If you want to use headphones to listen to music from your computer, you plug them into this jack.

Memory Card Reader

A memory card can be added to your laptop to increase your RAM storage or even replace your hard drive. These cards are small and are easy to install in a slot in your laptop, but can offer a lot of storage capacity.

Ethernet Jack

An Ethernet jack is used to connect your computer to a router that controls your local area network (LAN) through a coaxial or fiber-optic cable. You also use an Ethernet connection for a high-speed connection to the Internet such as a Digital Subscriber Line (DSL); you plug the cable into your laptop, and then connect the other end to a cable modem that is in turn connected to your phone line.

Modem Jack

If you use a phone to dial up your Internet connection, you can plug a phone cable into this jack to pick up a signal.

Monitor Port

If you want to connect an external monitor to your laptop, for example, to show a presentation on a larger screen, you can connect a standard monitor cable into the monitor port.

Understanding Hard Drives

Your computer can have several drives. All but the hard drive are removable or external. You can configure your hard drive to store data in the most efficient way for you.

Hard Drives

The hard drive (also called hard disk) is a hard platter in your laptop chassis. It is called a hard drive to distinguish it from softer floppy disks that were used to store data on a thin film. To store more data, many computers use hard drives with multiple disks.

How Data Is Stored

A hard drive uses magnetic recording to store your data, much like a cassette tape does. You can write data to a hard drive or erase it, although the magnetic pattern of data may stay on the drive long after you have erased it. Data is stored on the hard drive in files as a series of bytes.

Sectors and Tracks

When you store data in the form of files on your hard drive, it is saved in sectors within a series of tracks. Each sector contains a certain number of bytes, such as 256 or 512. When you format a disk, you are essentially creating the track and sector structure along with a file allocation table that is used for retrieving the data.

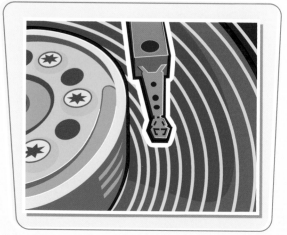

Read/Write Heads

In addition to the hard platter forming the hard drive, your laptop contains an 'arm' that holds read/write heads. When the hard drive spins, the heads move over the platter to locate the bytes that make up your file.

continued

Partitions

You can create partitions on a hard drive that essentially break it up into two or more hard drives. You may do this to run different operating systems on the same computer. You may also partition your data from your operating system so that if your operating system is damaged, your data remains safe.

How Data Is Retrieved

Whenever you access data, whether by opening a piece of software or opening a file, the read/write heads move across the hard disk, looking for the required bytes, which may be located in various sectors of the drive.

RAM

Computer memory that takes the form of a memory cell is referred to as random access memory (RAM). When your computer retrieves data from the hard drive, it picks up bytes that are stored non-sequentially (in different sectors) on the disk—hence the term *random access*. RAM comes in various types that work somewhat differently, such as dynamic random access memory (DRAM) or double data rate two (DDR2) synchronous DRAM.

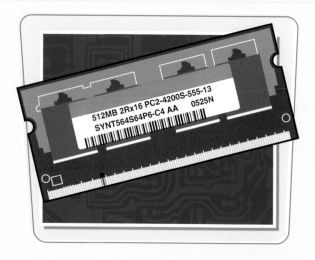

Hard Drive Capacity

Hard drives today have a certain capacity for storing data, measured in gigabytes (GB). In recent years, hard drives have grown to 160GB or more in size, with the most recent models packing as much as 500GB, although you can find laptops with as low as 20GB or 40GB capacity. The more you need to store and the more programs you need to run, the larger-capacity hard drive you should get.

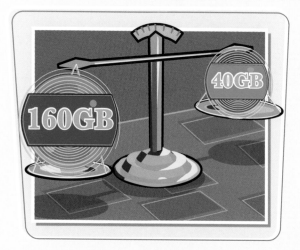

There are several types of media available for you to store copies of your data. You may do this to move the data to another computer, to give it to another person, or to keep a copy in case your hard drive is damaged.

Back Up Data

It is always a good practice to back up the data on your laptop. This provides you with a copy that is very useful if your hard drive is damaged, crashes, or is attacked by a computer virus. Remember that eventually, all hard drives will wear out; backing up data is insurance against that day.

CDs

CDs are hard plastic disks that are used to store data, music, or images. To read from or write to a CD, your laptop has to have a CD drive with the appropriate format (read, write, or read/write). Most laptops only have room for either a CD or a DVD drive, but not both. You can buy an external CD or DVD drive that you can connect to your laptop through a USB port.

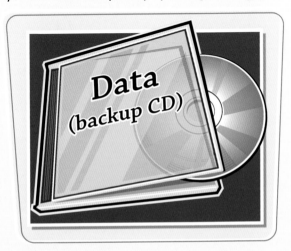

DVDs

DVDs are similar to CDs, but they have seven times the storage capacity of the average CD. In addition, video stored on DVD has a better picture quality. There have been several types of DVD format, and your laptop must have the corresponding DVD drive to run each type. The formats include +, -, and +/-. DVDs also come as readable, writeable, or read/write.

Flash Drives

A flash drive, also referred to as a USB stick or pen drive, is the size of a pack of gum, but can hold a huge amount of data. Flash memory is a type of solid-state chip that is also used in equipment such as digital cameras. You plug a flash drive into a USB port on your laptop, and so no special driver is required.

Understanding Power Options

Laptops have to carry their power supply with them when you take them on the road. They do this in the form of batteries. Laptop batteries come in various types. The time you can run your laptop on a charged battery is called the battery life, and this varies from laptop to laptop.

Batteries

Batteries provide a certain number of hours of battery life. The average laptop battery offers anywhere from two hours to four hours of battery life. The life of a battery is affected by whether the laptop is being used or is on standby, and by the size of the laptop display, with larger displays draining power more quickly than smaller ones.

Types of Batteries

There have been several types of laptop batteries, with the most recent type being lithium ion (Li-ion). Li-ion batteries hold a charge longer than earlier types such as nickel cadmium (NiCad) or nickel-metal hydride (NiMH).

Charging a Battery

You will need to charge your laptop battery on a regular basis. You do this by plugging the power cord of your computer into an electrical outlet. It is a good idea to let your battery drain almost completely before recharging it, as some older types of batteries will not work as efficiently over time if you do not follow this procedure.

Run on AC Power

If you are using your laptop at your home or office rather than on the road, you can plug it into an electrical outlet and run off of electricity all the time. However, laptops that are used for more than a few hours can become warm, and so you may want to invest in a laptop pad that helps to disperse heat.

Understanding Microprocessors

The microprocessor, or simply processor, that is inside your laptop enables the computer to run calculations and process data.

What a Microprocessor Does

A microprocessor includes logic circuitry that is used for performing calculations, as well as memory where data required for running your computer can be stored.

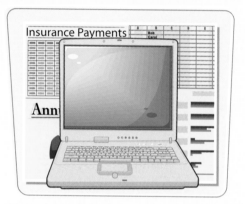

Microprocessor Design

Microprocessors come in the form of a computer chip. Built on a silicon wafer base, computer chips include an integrated circuit that is composed of millions of transistors.

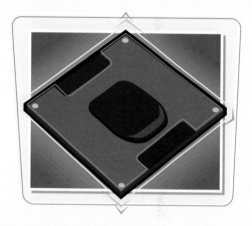

Types of Microprocessors

Microprocessors are built by several different companies, including Intel, IBM, and AMD. Today's most advanced microprocessors, called dual core, are actually two microprocessors on a single chip.

Microprocessor Clock Speed

You will often see a rating, expressed in gigahertz, for how fast the processor in your laptop runs. The faster the processor, the faster your computer operations are completed.

Choosing Laptop Peripherals and Accessories

Laptops are compact computers by definition, and they sometimes sacrifice some functionality to save on space. As a result, you sometimes need to attach other equipment to get things done. Attached or external equipment is referred to as *peripherals*. In addition, accessories such as a laptop case can make your life easier and protect your investment.

Get Extra Connectors

When you travel with your laptop, carrying certain cables and adapters may help you stay connected.

Connect on the Road

If you use a dial-up connection to go online, you may want to bring a phone cable with you. Some hotel phones have a line-out jack where you can plug in the cable and connect it to your laptop without having to disconnect the existing phone cable. If you have a wireless-enabled laptop, most hotels offer a wireless hot spot at no charge.

USB and Firewire Cables

It can be useful to carry a USB connector, because many peripheral devices, such as printers or external drives, connect through USB. Apple's interface for high-speed connections is called Firewire; several PCs are using a similar connection such as Sony's i.Link. Multimedia producers prefer Firewire to USB for connecting devices like microphone preamps and digital video cameras.

Travel Adapters

If you travel internationally, check into the type of electric adapter that you may need in your destination country. Without such an adapter, you could seriously damage your laptop when you plug it into a wall outlet to charge the battery.

Data Transfer Cables

If you want to back up your data to another computer, a data transfer cable can come in handy. This type of cable allows you to plug into each computer and directly transfer files between them.

Your laptop comes with a mouse and keyboard built in, but sometimes it is easier to work with a different input device. There are several devices available from online vendors and computer supply stores.

Stylus

If you use a Tablet PC, it comes with a stylus to write on the screen. Many people like to buy an extra stylus and take it with them on the road in case the first one is lost or mislaid. You can buy a stylus from your laptop manufacturer or in any office supply store for a few dollars.

Keyboards

You can connect a desktop keyboard to your laptop if you want an ergonomic keyboard or one that includes a number pad. You can also connect a virtual keyboard, which is a small device that projects a keyboard on a flat surface using laser technology. You can 'type' on whatever surface you like, using this device. Most keyboards of this kind require Bluetooth technology.

Joystick

If you enjoy gaming on your laptop, you may want a game controller or joystick. This provides controls to move around your game or fire virtual weapons. You can get one from most discount stores for $15 or less.

Wireless Mouse

Many people have difficulty getting used to a touchpad or button mouse on their laptops. If you find a traditional mouse easier to use, you can purchase a wireless mouse. These are slightly smaller than a traditional mouse. You plug a transmitter into a USB port, which controls the mouse without the need for cables.

A laptop case can help you carry your laptop easily while on the road, but it serves a more important purpose. It protects your laptop from dents and more serious damage if you drop it while on the run.

Laptop Briefcases

Laptop cases can resemble briefcases with extra padding and pockets to protect your investment and provide spaces for cables and storage discs.

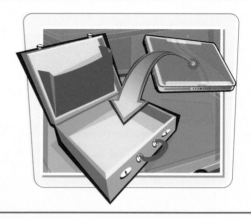

Laptop Sleeves

A laptop sleeve is a lighter-weight, slim, portfolio-style holder for your laptop, usually made of nylon or some other lightweight material. Note that many sleeves have no handle or strap to carry them by.

Laptop Backpacks

A backpack-style laptop holder keeps your hands free as you travel. This style provides a lot of extra space for cables or peripheral devices such as a portable printer.

Laptop Messengers

A popular style of laptop holder is the messenger bag, which resembles bags that bicycle couriers sling over their backs while riding their bikes around cities. These are usually made of lightweight nylon.

Wheeled Laptops

Especially if you carry a larger laptop, a case with a long handle and wheels can be a great asset. Instead of carrying your laptop, you can wheel it around the airport or on streets.

Fashion Laptop Bags

Laptop cases designed for the fashion-conscious traveler may look like a stylish handbag or tote bag. These are often marketed to women travelers who want a smart leather case.

Types of External Data Storage

Your laptop probably came with some kind of storage drive, such as CD or DVD. However, you may find that you need an additional form of data storage to store larger amounts of data more efficiently. You can use a peripheral or online storage service to help you store your data.

External CD/DVD Drive

In some situations, you may want to buy an external drive. For example, your laptop may only have a CD drive but you need to install software from a DVD, or your DVD drive may be readable but not writable. These external drives can be easily connected to your laptop through a USB port.

Flash Drive

A flash drive, or USB stick, can provide a lot of storage in a small package. Plugging one into a USB port is like adding a second hard drive. They come with different amounts of memory, from 256MB to 8GB. These drives are a lot pricier than a CD or DVD; expect to pay as much as $150 for the largest-capacity flash drives.

Portable Hard Drive

If you need to back up large amounts of data, you can buy a small portable hard drive (around 2 inches in size) that can provide many gigabytes or even terabytes of backup storage. These drives from manufacturers such as Fujitsu and Maxtor, spin at 5,400 rpm and can be powered by your laptop's Firewire or USB port.

Online Backup Services

One final option that makes a lot of sense for those who travel with a laptop is an online backup service. You can store data from any location with a broadband Internet connection, and retrieve that data from anywhere.

Most data storage devices simply plug into a USB port. You can then access them using Windows Explorer. In versions of Windows prior to Vista, you had to follow a procedure to safely remove hardware, but with Vista, you can simply pull the USB connector out.

Save to a Data Storage Device

1 Right-click the **Start** button (   ) on the Windows desktop.

2 Click **Explore**.

3 Right-click the folder or file that you want to save.

4 Click **Send to**.

5 Click the drive onto which you want to save the file or folder.

A progress window shows that the item is being copied to your storage drive.

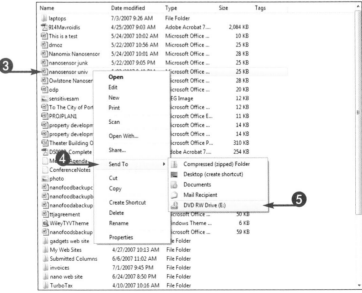

Add PC Cards

A PC card is a credit card-sized object that fits in a PC card slot on your laptop. PC cards can offer different functionality, such as a network antenna or security device.

Discover PC Cards

PC cards became popular with laptop users because they are small and durable. Because it is not advisable for users to open the chassis of a laptop, it is harder to insert added memory, sound cards, and other add-ons into your computer. PC cards are a way for you to add items from outside of your laptop. They are used for a wide variety of devices, including radio tuners, digital cameras, wireless phone connections, wireless LAN routers, and sound cards.

Types of PC Cards

There are three standard types of PC cards. Type I PC Cards are usually used for memory devices (for example, RAM, Flash, and SRAM (Static Random Access Memory) cards). Type II PC Cards are most often input/output (I/O) devices such as data/fax modems. Type III PC Cards are used when thicker components are required (for example, mass storage devices). Extended cards add components that have to extend outside the system to function, such as antennas for wireless capability.

Insert a PC Card

PC cards simply slip into a slot on the side of your computer. Some cards act as an interface to another device; in that case, a cable plugs into the part of the card extending out of the laptop, and connects to the device.

Remove a PC Card

Some PC cards slide completely into the slot on your computer; others extend outside the slot. To remove any PC card, push a release button next to the slot and it pops out. Never try to yank a card out of a slot without pushing the release button.

Add Memory

Rather than slotting a memory card into a desktop CPU, you can pop a memory PC card into the slot on your laptop. With the appearance of flash drive sticks, these cards may disappear, but if you have an older laptop with few USB ports, this option might come in handy.

Add Security Devices

You can add a fingerprint reader, also referred to as a biometrics card, to your laptop so that only you can log on. Security tokens also come in PC card format; these contain digital signatures that you can use to secure your data.

Work with Networks

A popular use of PC cards is to add a network airbus or antenna to your laptop to help you pick up a wireless network signal. If you purchase this type of card, be sure that it works with network security measures turned on.

Add Sound or Video

Laptop sound cards can upgrade your sound system to support Dolby digital features. These cards usually feature input and output jacks for connecting headphones. Some also feature connections to high-end speakers. Laptop video-capture cards typically allow you to receive TV signals on your laptop and to capture video images.

You can connect your laptop to any printer through a serial or USB cable, depending on the type of connection the printer supports. You can also buy a portable printer that is very small and lightweight. These typically use thermal or inkjet technology.

Connect to a Printer

INSTALL A PRINTER DRIVER

1 Place the disc that came with your printer in your CD or DVD drive.

Note: If you have no CD or DVD drive, proceed to the Step section, Connect to a Printer.

2 When a dialog box appears, click to proceed.

Note: The window that appears will vary depending on the software being installed.

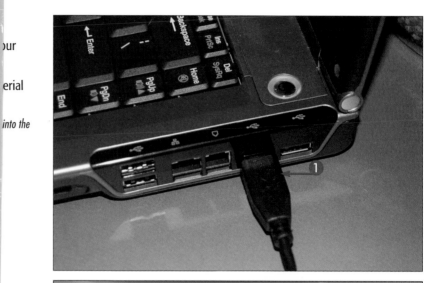

Installing device driver software ✕
Click here for status.

9:35 AM

our

erial

into the

e

alloon

a

ply

eps of the New Hardware Wizard
locate my printer's driver. What

otain the driver from your printer
easiest way to do that is to simply
turer's Web site and download

The following is printed on an overlaid book cover:

Choosing Books

0 – 1 YEAR
Close up photos of babies.
Touch and feel books.

1 – 2 YEARS
Sturdy books with only a
few words per page.
Lift-the-flap books.

2 – 3 YEARS
Books with rhymes, rhythms,
and repeating words.
About food, animals, trucks.

4 – 5 YEARS
More complex stories
and pictures.
Word games, repeating
language, predictable stories.

Because your laptop is portable, you can carry it wherever you go. That can be very convenient, but it also puts you at risk of having your laptop stolen or having others access your private information.

Understanding Security

When you think of security, you typically think of passwords and firewalls. These are important, and a device such as a fingerprint sensor can help to keep your data secure on the road. However, there are other security devices that you can use to keep strangers' hands off your laptop.

Cable Locks

You can attach your laptop to any object, such as a desk or a bolted-down chair in an airport, to deter anyone from a snatch-and-grab style theft. Most cable locks come with a combination-style lock, and attach through a lock slot that is available on most laptops.

Sensors and Alarms

There are many types of alarms. One type warns you if you are straying too far from your laptop. You carry a receiver that goes off when you move too far from the transmitter that you place with the laptop. PC card alarms fit in your PC card slot and set off an alarm if somebody picks up your computer. Mac laptops can use motion sensors built into the hard drive and a program called iAlertU to set off an alarm if the laptop is moved.

Fingerprint Sensors

Fingerprint sensors are used to restrict access to data on your laptop. Some laptop manufacturers are building fingerprint sensor technology right into the palm-rest area of their laptops. If yours is not equipped with one, you can buy a PC card fingerprint sensor that uses a small camera to capture and upload an image of your fingerprint to your computer, where it is checked against a stored fingerprint.

Two accessories are useful if you use your laptop at home. One keeps your laptop from overheating if you leave it on for hours at a time. The other makes it simple to connect your laptop to all kinds of at-home peripherals.

Your Laptop Off Road

When you use a laptop at your office or home instead of on the road, you may leave it turned on for much longer than the two- or three-hour battery life that you use while traveling. In addition, you are likely to want to connect the laptop to peripherals, such as a high-speed connection, printer, scanner, and so forth. Cooling pads and docking stations help in this situation.

Cooling Pads

Cooling pads use fans to cool the area under your laptop. Some plug right into your laptop, while others have to be plugged into an electrical outlet. Some cooling pads also raise your laptop to provide airflow underneath, further cooling the chassis.

Docking Stations

Docking stations can turn a portable laptop into a desktop computer solution without a lot of extra cabling. A laptop slots into the station, which contains a good supply of expansion slots, keyboard and mouse connectors, and USB slots. You can leave your peripherals plugged into the docking station, and then just place your laptop into the station to be up and running.

Port Replicators

A port replicator is similar to a docking station, in that it provides connections for peripherals such as a mouse, monitor, or printer. However, unlike a docking station, a port replicator does not include slots for expansion boards or storage devices.

Take Along Power Accessories

One accessory for laptops that some users cannot live without is a spare battery to extend their battery life on the road. In addition, although your laptop comes with a power cord (called an adapter), you may need a second one at some point.

Kinds of Batteries

Laptops come with different types of batteries, including lithium-ion (Li-ion) and nickel cadmium (NiCad). Check your manual to find out what kind of battery your model uses.

Travel with Batteries

Be aware that a spare battery can be heavy. If you find that you constantly need extra battery life when you travel, consider getting a model with longer battery life when buying your laptop. Look for a battery that has a higher mili-amperes per hour (mAH) number, such as 4400, for longer battery life.

Buy a Spare Battery

You will have to get a second battery that fits your laptop model chassis, and so you probably will have to buy it directly from your manufacturer or from an online store that carries laptop batteries of various makes. Be sure to get the right model battery, or it will not work.

Extra Adapters

Your laptop comes with a power cord, but if you lose it, damage it, or it does not work anymore, you can buy a replacement. Again, you must find an adapter that works with your make and model of laptop. Visit Web sites such as www.laptopsforless.com or your manufacturer's Web site to find the right adapter.

Adding headphones to your laptop is easy to do, and ensures that you can listen to music and more as you travel.

Using Headphones

Most laptops have built-in speakers. Still, when you travel with a laptop, headphones can be a great way to cut down on sound around you. In addition, if you want to listen to audio CDs or radio, or other types of sound files, headphones keep your listening experience private.

Headphone Styles

Inexpensive clip-on, earbud, and ear-canal headphones use small plugs that fit in your ear. Earpad-style headphones fit over your ear, placing a small speaker next to your ear canal. Full-size headphones are similar to earpad models, but they have slightly larger pads that cover your ears completely. For listening to your laptop speakers in a noisy area such as an airport or airplane, full-size headphones work best to block ambient noise. If you need to record sound, you will need headphones with a microphone attached.

Wireless Headphones

Wireless headphones use a base that transmits a signal in addition to the receiving headphones. Because of this set up, they are probably less suited to travel with your laptop, because the base itself is somewhat bulky to carry. Also, wireless reception is sometimes poor, and so these headphones are probably best used when your laptop is in a quieter area such as your home.

Connect a Headphone

Your laptop will have a headphone jack that is likely to have a small headphone symbol above or below it. Just plug the connector at the end of the headphone cable into the jack.

Connect and Test a Microphone

If you record sound files, such as narrations for PowerPoint presentations, you need a microphone.

Connect and Test a Microphone

1 Plug the microphone or headset with microphone into the microphone jack on your laptop.

2 Click .

3 Click **Control Panel**.

The Control Panel window appears.

4 Click **Hardware and Sound**.

Windows displays items in the Hardware and Sound category.

5 Click **Manage Audio Devices**.

Windows displays the Sound dialog box.

6 Click the **Recording** tab.

7 Click the **Microphone** device.

8 Click **Configure**.

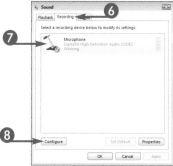

TIPS

I have a slightly older laptop and the steps for configuring the microphone do not match these.

The steps here are for Windows Vista laptops. Windows XP has slightly different categories in the Control Panel. With a MacBook, you would use the Sound pane, which you access through System Preferences.

I have a headphone with an attached microphone and only one plug. Do I plug it into the microphone jack?

No. Plug it into the headphone jack. Both the headphones and microphone are controlled by that connection. There are headphone/microphone combinations that have twoplugs, in which case one goes in the microphone jack and one into the headphone jack.

continued

When you connect a microphone, it is a good idea to make sure that it is working properly. To do this, you use the microphone setup wizard. Be sure to place the microphone directly in front of your mouth to test it so that it picks up your voice clearly.

Connect and Test a Microphone *(continued)*

⑨ Click **Set Up Microphone**.

Configure your Speech Recognition experience

Start Speech Recognition
Start using your voice to control your computer.

Set up microphone
Set up your computer to work properly with Speech Recognition.

Take Speech Tutorial
Learn to use your computer with speech. Learn basic commands and dictation.

Train your computer to better understand you
Read text to your computer to improve your computer's ability to understand your voice. Doing this isn't necessary, but can help improve dictation accuracy.

Open the Speech Reference Card
View and print a list of common commands to keep with you so you always know what to say.

If you would like to learn more about speech related tools and support from Microsoft, please visit the Microsoft Speech Online Community.

The "Configure your Speech Recongnition experience" page appears.

⑩ Click to select the type of microphone that you have (◯ changes to ◉).

⑪ Click **Next** three times to move through the initial wizard screens.

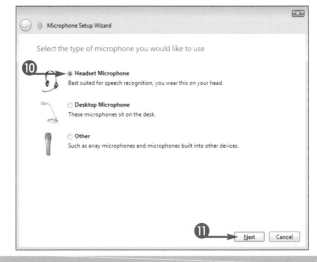

Microphone Setup Wizard

Select the type of microphone you would like to use

⊙ Headset Microphone
Best suited for speech recognition, you wear this on your head.

○ Desktop Microphone
These microphones sit on the desk.

○ Other
Such as array microphones and microphones built into other devices.

Next   Cancel

⑫ In the Adjust the Microphone Volume dialog box, read the sample sentences.

⑬ Click **Next**.

Note: If the wizard tells you that it could not hear your speech, check the connection of your microphone to your laptop and read the sentences again.

⑭ In the final dialog box, click **Finish** to complete the setup.

I have checked my connection and I am speaking into the microphone, but the computer is not picking up my voice. Can you offer any suggestions?

Your computer sound system could be muted. This can happen when you press a mute button on your keyboard, or click the **Mute** check box (☐ changes to ☑) in the volume setting on your Windows taskbar or in the System Volume dialog box. Check any of these settings to turn off the mute feature.

Are there any laptops that come with a built in microphone?

Yes. Look for a laptop like the MacBook or Dell XPS M1210 that has a built-in camera for Web conferencing. These typically also include a built-in microphone.

Buying Your Laptop

There are many styles of laptops available, from those designed to be lightweight and portable to heavy desktop models with large screens and hefty keyboards. The prices for laptops also vary widely, from around $600 to as much as $5,000. This chapter is where you discover all of the factors that are involved when choosing the perfect laptop for your needs and your pocketbook.

Choose an Operating System

An operating system is the software that makes your computer work. It comes pre-installed on any computer that you buy, and your laptop cannot operate without it!

What Is an Operating System?

An operating system (also called an OS) is the software that runs all of your applications, such as word processors and spreadsheets. In addition, an OS helps you manage your folders and files. OS security features help to keep your computer and data safe. You can use maintenance tools supplied by your operating system to repair or troubleshoot problems with your hardware and software. The two most commonly available operating systems in the world today are Windows and the Macintosh OS.

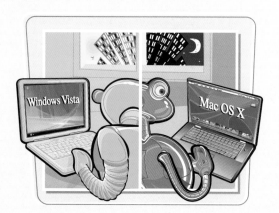

What Extras Come with an Operating System?

Although the main task of an operating system is to run applications and manage files, these systems also include extras such as games and small applications that allow you to perform basic tasks such as creating documents or calculating numbers. Accessibility features, such as magnification software for those with visual challenges, are also built into operating systems.

Which Version Should I Buy?

Operating systems are updated every few years, and so you should be sure that your laptop comes with the most current version. Around the time a new system is released, stores often sell off machines with the older system at enticing prices. If you buy a used laptop, you may also be buying an older operating system. You should compare features of the different versions to be sure that the newest system is worth the extra money.

Upgrading Your Operating System

At some point in time, manufacturers stop supporting an older operating system. If you buy a laptop with an older version of an operating system and you want to upgrade to the latest version, go to a computer store or the manufacturer's Web site and look for an upgrade version. The upgrade version costs much less than the full product.

Microsoft Windows

The most popular operating system in the world today is Windows from Microsoft. Microsoft Windows Vista is the most current version of this operating system, which is built into computer models from a wide variety of manufacturers, including Dell, Gateway, and Toshiba. Windows comes in several versions designed for home or business users. Check the features in each product to be sure that you get the one that meets your needs.

Apple Macintosh

The other commonly available OS only comes installed on computers from Apple, Inc. Apple Macintosh OS X v.10.5 Leopard is the most recent version of this operating system, which you can currently find on the MacBook and MacBook Pro laptops. One interesting note is that you can buy software that allows an Apple computer to operate both Windows and the Macintosh OS on a single computer.

Select a Price Range

The price of your laptop depends on several factors. You are the only person who can decide which features are most important to you, and what your budget should be.

Consider the Source

You can buy a laptop from a discount store or the manufacturer, and prices vary accordingly. You can often have a less expensive laptop custom-made by a company that builds products from parts that they obtain from different sources. You can pay a bit more to buy a name-brand computer, or to get special warranties or follow-up support from a manufacturer. You can even buy a computer from an auction site, such as eBay; in this case, you would be dealing with individuals or small businesses that are unfamiliar to you, although many are reputable. Price should be weighed against your comfort with the seller and their ability to support you after the sale.

Features

Features that affect the price of a laptop include the brand, version, and speed of the processor; the amount of available memory; battery life; size of the monitor; and its ability to handle graphics. Several of these features are covered in more detail in this chapter. Remember that you should only spend money on features that you need. Do not buy a feature that you do not really need, such as a fancy graphics card. Also remember that you can upgrade some features of a laptop after you buy it, if your needs change.

Select the Right Weight

Laptops started out as portable computing devices for people who spent a great deal of time traveling. Today you can find ultra-portable laptops that weigh as little as 2 pounds, but you can also buy a desktop laptop that weighs as much as 18 pounds. With laptops becoming more affordable and including multimedia features and larger screen sizes, many people are adopting them as stay-at-home models.

Portability

If you need a laptop to get work done while on the road, you should consider lighter-weight laptops. These range in weight from a couple of pounds to seven or eight pounds. There is sometimes a tradeoff in features and price when you buy a very light-weight laptop. A two-pound laptop may be more expensive, and may be less able to handle larger programs or run at faster speeds. A larger portable laptop may offer more speed or features, but it may be difficult to carry on long trips.

Stay-at-Home Laptops

Some people are beginning to use laptops at home. They take up less space than a computer tower, and it is easier to plug external devices into them without having to crawl around on the floor or turn around a heavy tower. Although weight is less of an issue in this situation, consider whether you might want to carry such a computer from room to room on a regular basis before you choose the heaviest model.

Look at Wireless Capabilities

Wireless computing offers you the ability to connect to the Internet to communicate from almost anywhere without cable connections or a phone line. If you are taking your laptop on the road, the ability to connect to wireless networks while traveling, or at your destination, can be very important.

How Wireless Works

There are wireless devices, such as a wireless mouse, that work by transmitting a one-way radio signal. There is also the wireless Internet, which requires a wireless card or device and an Internet access point for two-way communication. You can subscribe to Wireless Wide Area Network (WWAN) services from popular providers such as Cingular and Verizon to pick up their signal when you travel. You can also take advantage of wireless 'hot spots' in restaurants, airports, and hotels to connect for free or for a fee. The transmission speed for wireless networks varies, depending on the quality of the connection, and the wireless device installed in your laptop.

Wireless Laptops

When you buy a laptop, you should make sure that it includes wireless technology. There have been several versions of wireless technology protocols, including Bluetooth and WiFi, also referred to as 802.11. WiFi versions include a, b, and g, with the most recent version being 802.11n. Equipment rated for wireless version n boosts your wireless range significantly. If your computer does not include wireless capability, you can also insert a wireless connection SIM card (sometimes called an air card) into a slot in your laptop to obtain it.

If you take your laptop on the road, battery life is important. Battery life represents the number of hours your computer can operate on a fully charged battery.

How Many Hours Do You Need?

Some desktop-model laptops offer under an hour of battery life because you can keep them plugged into your power source. Some so-called road warrior laptops offer as much as four or more hours of battery life. Choose the battery life rating that fits how and where you use your laptop.

What Affects Battery Life

Battery life depends on the type of battery, and how you are using your laptop. A large monitor display drains a battery faster. If you keep your computer in standby mode, your battery will not drain as quickly as if you are actively working with software or an online connection. Your battery might also be affected by extreme weather conditions.

Choose the Best Battery

There are different types of batteries and new ones are coming along all the time. Knowing the latest battery technology before you buy can help you get a laptop that will serve you for years to come.

Battery Types

Batteries are being improved all the time to provide longer battery life at lighter weights. As of this writing, the latest type of battery is Lithium ion, or Li-ion. Although light and able to hold a charge for a long time, this battery type is expensive. Nickel metal hydride, or NiMH, batteries are still common in laptops today and less expensive than Li-ion, but they can suffer from something called *memory effect*, which can cause the battery to be less efficient. Nickel cadmium, or Ni-Cd, batteries can be powerful but have even more problems with memory effect. To overcome memory effect, you can let the battery run down to empty before recharging.

Add a Second Battery

One option to extend your battery life is to carry a second charged battery with you; when the first one runs low, simply swap them out. You have to purchase an additional battery, and it adds weight to what you have to carry on the road, but it may be worth it to you to extend your available working time.

Laptop displays range in size from a tiny five inches to 20 inches. These displays can also vary in the quality of their image. The monitor that you need depends on how many hours you will spend in front of it and what functions you need to perform.

Display Size

If you mainly need to check e-mail and type a few documents on the road, a smaller monitor might be adequate. However, if you spend hours reading reports, studying graphs, and viewing high-end graphics, a larger monitor is best. Of course, monitor size affects portability, with larger monitors best suited for a desktop-model laptop.

Display Quality

Laptop monitors use liquid crystal displays, or LCDs, and they vary widely in quality. You will hear various terms such as backlit and reflective, active matrix and passive matrix, and TFT. Generally speaking, TFT active-matrix, backlit displays are superior for use in laptops. You should check the screen resolution, which refers to the number of pixels that form an image on the screen. The higher the numbers are, the crisper the display. These days, you should look for a resolution of at least 1024 x 768 pixels, and much higher if you use graphics-intensive applications.

Keep in mind that laptop monitors are notoriously fragile. Avoid scratching them or submitting them to extreme temperatures.

Determine Memory and Storage Needs

Your computer needs a certain amount of random access memory, or RAM, to run programs and load files. More memory can also help your computer run faster. Your hard drive is where you store data.

RAM

RAM is the memory required to access data and run programs. The more RAM your system has, the faster items load on your computer. There have been several varieties of RAM chips, including dynamic random access memory (DRAM) and synchronous dynamic random access memory (SDRAM), as well as the latest variety, double-data-rate 2 synchronous dynamic random access memory (DDR2). RAM chips are rated by their maximum clock rate — which relates to how quickly they can request data to appear — and by their memory size. RAM chip speed is measured in megahertz (MHz), and its size is measured in megabytes (MB) or gigabytes (GB).

Hard Drive Capacity

You should buy a hard drive with enough capacity to handle your day-to-day data storage needs. Remember that a 60GB hard drive is pretty much the minimum standard today. If you need more storage capacity, look for at least a 120GB hard drive. A faster hard-drive rotational speed (how fast it spins) of about 7,200 RPM can also be useful to power users and gamers.

Memory Card Readers

Your laptop may include a slot where you can insert a memory card to add to your system memory. You can add these memory cards after you buy your system if you find that your memory needs change.

Basic Requirements

Windows Vista requires 512MB of system memory (RAM) and a 20GB hard drive to run properly. Mac OS X requires a minimum of 256MB of RAM, and the smallest-capacity hard drive on any Mac laptop is currently 60GB.

Everyday Use

In reality, minimum requirements for operating systems are not enough for a smooth computing experience. If it fits in your budget, you should probably look for at least 1GB of RAM and an 80GB hard drive.

Power Users

You may need to run several programs at once (called multitasking). For example, you may want to check your e-mail while running a PowerPoint presentation and opening a Word document. In this case, you may want a little more memory than for everyday use.

Graphics and Gaming

For the graphics professional or hardcore gamer, look for 2GB of RAM, and a 120GB or greater hard drive. Also, the cache rating of your processor can translate into faster speeds, with 1MB being sufficient, and 4MB being a powerful feature that is desirable for these higher-end applications.

The microprocessor is the chip in your computer. The type of microprocessor that your laptop comes with can make a big difference in the speed of its performance.

Microprocessors

Microprocessors, or simply processors, are the brains of any computer, enabling it to perform calculations and process data. A microprocessor comes in the form of a computer *chip*. These chips are constantly being improved to include more processing power on a chip, handle multiple tasks concurrently, and generate less heat.

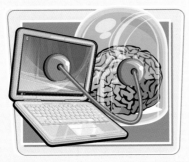

Brands of Microprocessors

Although Macintosh laptops used to come with an IBM processor chip, they have recently made the switch to Intel chips. For Windows-based PCs, Intel and their competitor AMD are the two biggest processor manufacturers.

Processor Efficiency

Older computers may have Pentium, Celeron M (standing for "mobile"), or Core Solo single-core chips, which did not use power efficiently. Intel recently introduced the Core 2 Duo, which, along with its predecessor the Core Duo, has two processors. AMD's latest offering is the Turion X2 Dual Core chip. These dual processors enable your computer to more efficiently run several tasks at once, at faster processing speeds (measured in GHz) and with lower power usage.

Choose a Microprocessor

If you need long battery life for a laptop that you travel with frequently, you might look for a Mobile Core 2 Duo, which uses less power (about 34 watts) while providing the advantages of dual processors. Whichever microprocessor you choose, look for a clock speed of at least 1GHz for processing efficiency.

Graphics cards (also called video cards) are what generate images on your display. They are particularly important when playing games or running animations.

Graphics Cards

Graphics cards contain a graphics processing unit (a GPU) with a specific speed and amount of memory. However, for most users, the graphics card that comes installed on a laptop is sufficient. The largest manufacturers and the ones that you are likely to see preloaded on your laptop are ATI, Intel, and NVIDIA.

Multimedia and Gaming

If you use graphics-rich applications, such as any design or animation software or games, the more memory and speed your graphics card has, the better. Your graphics card has to be a good match for your CPU; a very powerful graphics card with a slower or older CPU would be wasted. Also, be aware that not all graphics cards work on all computers. Be sure to check the frame rate if you are playing advanced video games, as lower rates can slow down video and animations.

Examine the Keyboard and Mouse

The keyboard and mouse are the tools that you use to interact with installed applications and the Internet. Laptops offer a variety of styles and a range of quality in keyboards and mouse devices. The choice often comes down to your own personal preference and comfort.

The Keyboard

The keyboards on laptops can vary from those that are condensed for space — depending on function keys to provide full functionality — to expansive, desktop-style keyboards with number pads and special shortcut keys. Your choice of keyboard is mostly related to the size and weight of laptop that you need.

Choosing a Keyboard

One of the most important features of a laptop is how the keyboard feels to you. If possible, try out the keyboard before you buy. If you are buying online, try to find any laptop model from the same manufacturer to test in person. The feel of the keys under your hands, the heat on your wrists as you rest them on the laptop case, and the size of the keyboard should all be important factors in your choice of laptop.

The Mouse

Laptops all have integrated mouse devices so that you can function without adding on equipment when you go on the road. If you like, you can attach a wireless mouse through a USB port to add more traditional mouse functionality to your laptop.

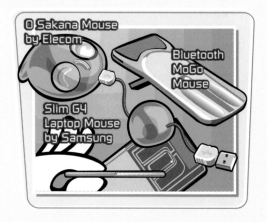

O Sakana Mouse by Elecom

Bluetooth MoGo Mouse

Slim G4 Laptop Mouse by Samsung

Laptop Mouse Options

Built-in mouse devices are typically of the touchpad or button variety. A touchpad allows you to pass your finger over a flat panel below the keyboard to move the mouse onscreen. A button is often embedded in the middle of the keyboard and requires that you press it with your finger. Both methods require some getting used to, and so you should try out both to see which comes more naturally to you.

Using a Corded or Wireless Mouse

There are several portable mouse devices on the market that can connect to your laptop via a USB port or via a wireless connection. These are smaller than your desktop mouse so they are easy to take with you when you travel with your laptop. Some even fit on a keychain.

When you are ready to buy your laptop, you will find that many stores and manufacturers offer you a mind-boggling array of adds-ons to choose from. Selecting the best options for your needs can keep the price down and get you the system you want.

Set a Budget

As you add extras to your purchase, you can quickly see a $999 system run up to $1,800 or more with added options. Sometimes it pays to start with a basic system and add features, and sometimes it makes sense to buy a loaded system for a higher price depending on your needs.

Pre-installed Software

Trial versions of programs such as Microsoft Office are usually pre-loaded on your computer. However, some free programs may be included. Look for a basic productivity suite such as Microsoft Works. It may save you time and money to have the manufacturer install other programs when they configure your system. Also, look for the most current version of an operating system, and if a new one is imminent, consider waiting for its release or buying a new version-compatible model.

Expandability

Although it is next to impossible to access the inside of your laptop and change out hard drives or swap out your monitor, you can expand certain features to ensure that your current system serves your future needs. Look for several USB slots where you can add memory modules or network adapter cards. You also need these slots to add peripherals such as an external DVD drive or printer.

Do Your Homework

Features and technologies change all the time. When they do, stores try to sell off the old technology at a discount. If you do not need the latest features, then this can be good news for you. However, if you buy a last-generation laptop today, it may too soon become obsolete, and unable to run the software that comes out a year after you buy it. Also check out the audio card and speakers if you need good quality sound.

Extras

When purchasing your laptop, you may want to pick up a few extra items, such as a laptop case; a docking station that you can plug into when you are using your laptop at home or the office; an extended warranty; a service agreement; or flash drives (also called USB sticks). These can add to the price, and may be less expensive from a discount computer store than from the laptop manufacturer.

Wear and Tear

There are several models of rugged laptops on the market. These models can be used in rugged terrain with somewhat extreme temperatures, and you can even drop them from a height of a few feet without damaging them. If you intend to take your laptop to the Sahara or a construction site, consider a rugged laptop model.

Tablet PCs

One variation on typical laptop forms is the tablet PC, available from several manufacturers. These models offer a legal pad-like design and the ability to "write" on the screen with a stylus using a technology called Ink. They are typically lightweight, and have features that allow you to transcribe handwriting into word-processed text. If you need portability and the ability to handwrite notes, a tablet PC might be for you.

Security

One other item that you might consider when buying a laptop is its security features. Today, laptops can come with everything, from your name engraved on the chassis to a locking cable and a wireless fingerprint sensor. If you are carrying secure data on your laptop, check into its available security features before you buy.

CHAPTER

4

Setting Up Your New Laptop

Charge Battery!

When you bring home a new laptop, there are some things that you need to do to get it charged up and connected, so that you can start to use it. This chapter guides you through these steps so that you are ready to get to work quickly.

If you have never owned a laptop computer, you should take a moment to get used to how the computer opens and closes, and how to take care of the screen. Models differ slightly in how the shells latch, but most work in a similar fashion.

Open the Laptop

Laptops typically latch on the front of the chassis with a slider mechanism. You move the slider to the right and the top releases. Do not force the top open or you may break the latch.

Open a Tablet PC

Tablet PCs come in two different styles. The clamshell variety looks like a standard laptop; you unlatch the slider to open it, and when you want to use it in Tablet PC mode, you swivel the monitor display to lay flat on the computer. With the other tablet PC type, there is nothing to open; the computer screen is like a pad that you can write directly on, and you can use an onscreen keyboard to input text or connect an external keyboard using a port.

Close the Laptop

Closing the lid of your laptop is simply a matter of pushing it shut. The slider mechanism automatically engages. If you are using a clamshell-style tablet PC, you have to swivel the screen back to a standard laptop configuration, and then close it.

Care for the Screen

Laptop screens are typically liquid crystal displays (LCDs). They are somewhat soft to the touch, and unfortunately can be damaged rather easily. For that reason, be careful not to scratch, poke, or somehow dent the screen or it may become unusable. Although it is possible to have your manufacturer replace the screen or to buy and install a replacement yourself, it is expensive to do this.

The location of connections for different cables varies, depending on your laptop model. Check the user's manual or setup sheet that came with your unit for specifics, if they are available.

Attach Devices

USB stands for universal serial bus, a small port that is used to connect a variety of devices, from monitors to printers. Most laptops provide several USB ports so that you can connect several devices at once. USB ports can also be used to insert flash drives that allow you to back up your computer files. In case your device cannot use a USB connector, some laptops also include a monitor port or serial port for a printer.

Connect a Phone Line or Network

Most laptops also provide a jack for plugging in a phone line to the internal modem to use a dial-up connection, and an Ethernet jack to connect to a wired network. An Ethernet jack looks similar to a phone jack, although it is slightly bigger.

PC Card Slots and Memory Card Readers

PC cards can be used to add memory or functionality, such as a fingerprint reader for laptop security. The slot is long and narrow, with a button to release the card when you want to take it out. A memory card reader looks like a smaller PC card slot. Memory card readers are often used to insert a storage card from a digital camera so that you can upload photos to your computer.

IEEE 1394 Port

Also called a FireWire (the term used by Apple, which developed the technology), IEEE 1394 connections are used for high-speed data transfer. IEEE 1394 connections are great for transferring video files to and from your laptop.

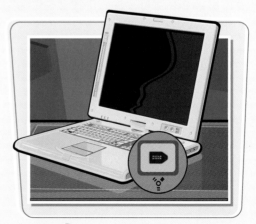

Charge the Battery

When you open the box containing your new laptop, the battery may or may not hold a charge. You can use it right away by connecting it to your wall outlet, but to use battery power only, you may have to charge the battery first.

Battery Life

When not plugged into an electrical outlet using a cord that comes with your laptop, your computer runs on battery power. Laptop batteries have what is called a *battery life* (that is, how long the computer runs before the battery is drained). Their battery life can be anywhere from a couple of hours to five or six hours.

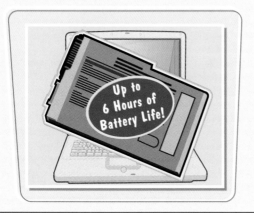

Avoid Battery Memory Effect

Some types of rechargeable batteries have a problem called a *memory effect*. This means that if you charge them when they are not completely or nearly drained, they may lose some of their battery life capacity. For this type of battery, it is important that you let it run down almost completely before charging it again. Check your user's manual for warnings about this effect with your model's battery. Most newer batteries do not experience the memory effect.

Charge the Battery

Charging your battery simply involves plugging the electrical cord that came with your laptop into a wall outlet. The charging time can vary, so consult your user's manual. With some older battery types, leaving the laptop plugged in after the battery is charged can damage the battery. Temperature can also affect battery charge time.

Take a Spare

Many people like to purchase and take along a spare battery to double the time that they have to work while on the road. It is usually easy to pop out one laptop battery and insert another. See your user's manual for instructions on how to do this on your computer model.

Turning a laptop on is pretty similar to turning on a desktop computer model. Once you find the On button, you press it! Putting laptops in sleep mode and turning them off may work slightly differently than with your desktop model.

The Power button on a laptop is typically located inside. Once you open the lid, look for a small button somewhere near the hinges of the laptop.

Turn the Laptop On and Off

TURN ON A LAPTOP

① Press the Power button.

In a few moments, the computer boots up and your operating system's welcome screen appears.

TURN OFF A LAPTOP

① To turn off a Windows-based laptop, click **Start** ( ).

② Click the **Power button** ( ).

*Note: If you have a Macintosh laptop, click the **Apple** icon, and then click **Shut Down**. In the dialog box that appears, choose **Shut Down**.*

Install a Program

When you begin to use your laptop, you may have to install software, from frequently used programs to device drivers that run peripheral devices such as a printer. This task covers installing a Windows-based program.

1 Insert your software disc into your internal or external CD or DVD drive.

Note: *In most cases, the software displays a window to guide you through the installation. If you have to install the software from the Internet, continue with the following steps.*

2 Open your Web browser and locate the program online using your browser Search feature.

Note: *See Chapter 11 for information about using your browser.*

3 Click the **Download Now** button or link.

Note: *If you are paying for the software, you may have to proceed through several screens to enter your credit card information.*

4 Click **Open** or **Run**.

The program downloads; you may have to follow directions to install the program once it is downloaded.

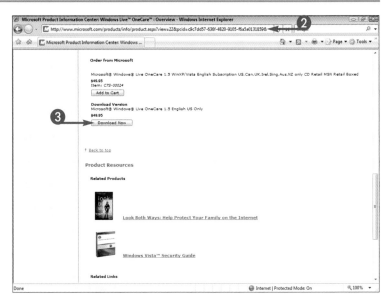

Although you can connect a traditional mouse to a USB port or by using wireless technology, the built-in mouse device on your laptop can deliver full mouse capabilities. The two common types of laptop mouse devices are the touchpad and the button mouse.

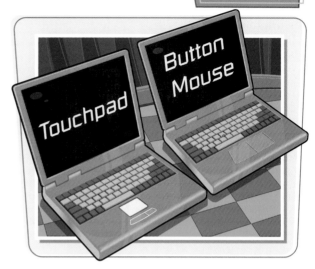

Use a Touchpad or Button Mouse

USE A TOUCHPAD

① Place your finger on the touchpad.

Note the position of the mouse cursor on your monitor.

② Slide your finger around the touchpad.

Note how the mouse cursor moves on the screen.

USE A BUTTON MOUSE

① Gently press your finger onto the button.

② Move your finger across the button.

Note how the onscreen cursor moves in sync with your finger.

● For laptops with either a touchpad or button mouse, you will have two large buttons somewhere beneath your keyboard that you can press for traditional left- and right-mouse button functions.

Input with a Tablet PC

A tablet PC uses different methods of input from a standard laptop. You can actually 'write' on the screen using a special device called a stylus. You can also use an onscreen keyboard to enter text and navigate around Windows.

Work with Ink

Tablet PCs use a technology from Microsoft called Ink, which allows you to write or draw on the computer screen. Whatever you input on the screen is transferred into a document in whatever application you have open at the time.

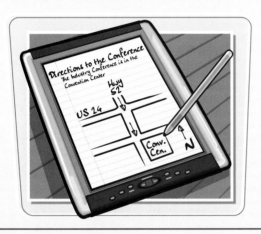

Stylus

A stylus for a tablet PC is not just a plastic stick, although it looks like one. It is actually an electromagnetic pen that enables it to send a digital signal through the screen. A stylus is included with your tablet PC, although you can buy additional ones from your manufacturer or a computer supply store.

Change Writing to Text

Tablet PC software often has an ink-to-text feature that allows you to select what you have written with the stylus and convert it to a regular computer font. In this way, you can handwrite notes or a report and then convert it to text.

Use the Onscreen Keyboard

Another way to input text or move around your tablet PC environment is to use an onscreen keyboard. Once it displays, you can 'type' on this keyboard using your stylus.

A wireless mouse is a natural addition to any laptop. It does not require cables, it is lightweight and easy to take along, and it replaces the sometimes awkward touchpad or button mouse on your laptop with the familiar functionality of the desktop mouse.

How a Wireless Mouse Works

When you plug a wireless mouse into your laptop, it overrides the built-in mouse function. You may have to install driver software for your wireless mouse model so that your computer knows how to run it.

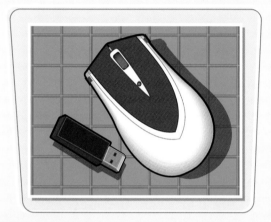

The Elements of a Mouse

There are different styles of mouse, but most today include a right and left button and a scroll wheel. The left button is used for clicking in a document to place your cursor, and clicking and dragging to select objects and text. The right button is used to display shortcut menus. The scroll button helps you scroll through documents by simply rolling the wheel.

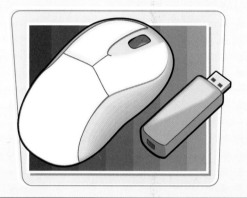

Choose the Mouse

You can find a wireless mouse specifically designed for laptop users. They are smaller than a traditional mouse, and so they are easy to fit in a tiny space such as an airplane seatback tray.

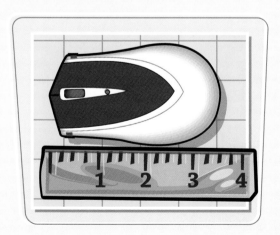

Make the Connection

The best style of wireless mouse for a laptop is one that connects to the laptop through a transmitter you insert into a USB port. You simply plug in the stick that comes with the mouse, and start using it.

Get to Know the Keyboard

In addition to the alphanumeric keys that you press to enter text, laptops often include specialized keys. For example, the Windows key is used to open the Windows Start menu on a laptop running Windows. Apple laptops include special Option and Command keys, which are pressed in combination with other keys as a shortcut to perform specific actions.

Modifying Keys

There are several keys on your keyboard that you use to modify actions. For example, **Shift**, **Ctrl**, and **Alt**, when pressed with another key, modify how that key works. **Ctrl** + **V** pastes copied text, and **Shift** plus a letter capitalizes the letter.

Navigation Keys

Because a laptop mouse can be hard to maneuver for some users, consider trying the following keys to navigate: **End**; **Home**; **Page up** and **Page down**; **Tab**; and the directional keys ⬇, ⬆, ⬅, and ➡.

Function Keys

Function keys are available on all keyboards to provide shortcuts to functions in programs. Function keys marked **F1** to **F12** initiate different actions, depending on the program you are working in. On a laptop where space is at a premium, there is often a key labeled **Fn**; by pressing this key along with a function key, you can initiate a different function than you would by pressing the function key alone.

Escape

The Escape key, labeled `Esc`, stops a current action and can be useful if you want to back out of an action or leave without saving an entry.

Caps Lock

The Caps Lock key turns the Caps Lock feature on and off. With Caps Lock on, anything that you type appears in uppercase. With Caps Lock off, everything that you type is lowercase, and you need to press `Shift` to capitalize a letter, such as the first letter of the first word in a sentence, or the word "I".

WITH CAPS LOCK ON, EVERYTHING YOU TYPE IS UPPERCASE

Enter, Spacebar, Delete, and Backspace

The `Enter` key is used to start a new paragraph in a text document or to accept an entry in a dialog box or a cell in a table. The `Spacebar` is used to add a space between letters in a sentence. Press `Delete` or `Del` to delete a selected object or text. Press `Backspace` to move your cursor back one letter.

Programmable Keys

Programmable keys are available on most keyboards for accessing the Internet or playing music. These keys can be programmed to perform different functions, but in most cases you should probably leave them at the manufacturer's settings to avoid confusion.

On your desktop keyboard, you probably have a numeric keypad to the far right. You can use this keypad if you are in an application where you need to enter a lot of numbers, such as a spreadsheet program.

How the Numeric Keypad Works

Because many people are used to entering numbers using a calculator or adding machine, the arrangement of numbers across the top of the keyboard can be difficult to use when you have to enter a lot of numbers. Therefore, most keyboards include a numeric keypad that resembles a calculator to speed number entry. To shift functionality to the numeric keypad, you press Num lock.

Examine the Embedded Numeric Keypad

On laptops, where space is limited, clever designers came up with a way of embedding the number pad functionality within the letter keys. When you turn on NumLock, pressing those keys turns them into numeric keypad keys.

Adjust Screen Brightness

You can adjust the brightness of your laptop screen. This allows you to have the best image in different lighting, such as in your office or on a darkened airplane.

Your Laptop Screen

Laptop screens are made up of small dots called pixels. Light coming from behind the screen passes through these pixels. Liquid crystals in the display (hence the name liquid crystal display or LCD) are modified by an electrical signal to adjust the color and brightness that you see. When you adjust screen brightness, you are actually changing the electric field and the alignment of those crystals.

Adjust Brightness

With most laptops, you adjust screen brightness using the Fn key in combination with a function key such as F8. Look for a function key that has a symbol of a little bright sun or something similar. However, note that the brighter the screen is, the greater the drain on your battery power.

CHAPTER 5

Working with a Macintosh

If you decide that a Macintosh is the best laptop for you, you will find that some things work in a similar way to Windows, but some things are different. In this chapter, you will discover some of the basics of using a MacBook or MacBook Pro and the Leopard operating system.

Unlike Windows-based computers, the MacBook and MacBook Pro laptops are only manufactured by Apple. This means that you do not have to choose among several brands, but you do get to choose the features you need.

Price

There is a big jump in price when you go from the MacBook to the higher-end MacBook Pro. Expect to spend around $1,000 for a basic MacBook and $1,800 to as much as $2,800 for a MacBook Pro, depending on the features you want to add. You can purchase directly from Apple, which never offers sale prices, or from distributors such as MacMall or MacConnection, where you may see rebates or savings of about $100 from Apple's prices. These third-party stores may also offer software bundles that will save you money.

Processor Power

Processor speed affects how fast your Mac runs applications. Recently, Apple switched to Intel processors, which have been one of the standard Windows processors for years. The most recent processor is an Intel Core 2 Duo, just like the one found in Windows laptops. As of this writing, you can choose a MacBook or MacBook Pro with speeds ranging from 2 to 2.4 GHz, with a cache as large as 4MB.

Mac Advantages

If you are weighing the pros and cons of buying a Mac, there are a few things to consider. There are far fewer viruses that can invade a Mac, both because it has strong security and because many more hackers target Microsoft than Apple. Macs come with just about every driver you need so that you do not have to download drivers for peripheral devices. Finally, Macs are known for being great computers for working with graphics and highly graphical game programs. You can save files in both Mac and Windows formats in most applications, although you may still have some file compatibility issues. However, one warning: it is tricky to set up a Mac to work on a PC-based home network.

Screen Size and Weight

MacBooks come with a 13-inch screen. MacBook Pros come with either a 15-inch or 17-inch screen. Of course, the larger screens bring with them added weight. For example, a 13-inch MacBook weighs a little over 5 pounds, while a 17-inch MacBook Pro weighs 6.8 pounds.

Included Programs

Macs come with a lot of useful programs, many of which are part of the iLife suite, such as iWeb for Web publishing, iPhoto for image manipulation, Address Book for contact management, and the Safari browser. Widgets provide a lot of smaller application functionality, such as a calculator, clock, and dictionary. If you want a suite of applications to get your work done, you can purchase iWorks or Microsoft Office for the Mac.

Run Windows Programs

In the past, it was difficult to run Windows files or programs on a Mac, but today, you can buy software that allows your Mac to run Windows Vista and other Windows programs. You can use a software program such as Bootcamp 1.3 or Parallels Desktop for Mac, along with a copy of Windows XP or Windows Vista, to run both the Mac and Windows operating systems on your MacBook or MacBook Pro.

Set Up
Your Mac

As with Windows-based computers, you can set up a lot of preferences for how your Mac works. You can do this through the System Preferences.

Get Started with Setup Assistant

The first time you start up your Mac laptop (by pressing the Power button), the Setup Assistant appears. Follow this easy-to-use procedure to set up a user account for your Mac, set up your Internet connection, and register with Apple.

Set System Preferences

You can access System Preferences by clicking the **Apple** menu icon (🍎) and choosing **System Preferences.** The System Preferences window has four major categories of settings: Personal, Hardware, Internet & Network, and System. Clicking any of the icons in these categories displays a pane with detailed settings.

Personal

The Personal category of settings allows you to set up the appearance of your screen, desktop, and the Dock. You can also control Exposé window management, what language your Mac uses, and security settings, and you can modify the order in which the Spotlight search feature displays results.

Hardware

Hardware settings help you to control your input devices, display, printers, faxes, sound, storage media, and wireless connections. Another very important hardware-related feature for laptop users is Energy Saver, which controls useful power management settings.

Internet & Network

The four items in this category of settings help you to set up a trial or paid membership with .Mac, an online hosted service from Apple that you can use for communicating and sharing files; set up your wireless or Ethernet network; set up QuickTime multimedia software architecture to play multimedia files; and control file sharing settings.

System

The settings in the System category help you to control user accounts, and specify settings for the date and time, accessibility, parental controls, and speech. You can also use features in this category to update your software, and manage the Time Machine file backup feature.

The Mac desktop is your central location for accessing applications, working with folders and files, and using a variety of useful tools called Widgets.

Menu Bar

The Menu Bar across the top of the desktop is where the currently open application's commands are located. If no application is open, then the Finder menus appear here. There is also an Apple menu that includes System Preferences and commands for tasks such as shutting off your system or putting it to sleep, updating your software, controlling the position of the Dock, and opening recently used documents and applications.

The Dock

The Dock contains icons representing various tools in your Mac. From here, you can launch the Safari browser, your Address Book, the Dashboard, Trash, and other programs.

Finder

The Finder is the equivalent of Windows Explorer. It is a window that allows you to access the contents of your computer, including your drives, folders, files, and applications. From this window, you can also create new folders and arrange desktop icons by various criteria.

Menu Bar Icons

On the right of the Menu Bar are a series of icons that let you access some common settings, such as your wireless connection, speaker volume, and date and time.

Desktop Icons

You can place programs, files, and folders on your desktop, and double-click them to manage or view them within windows.

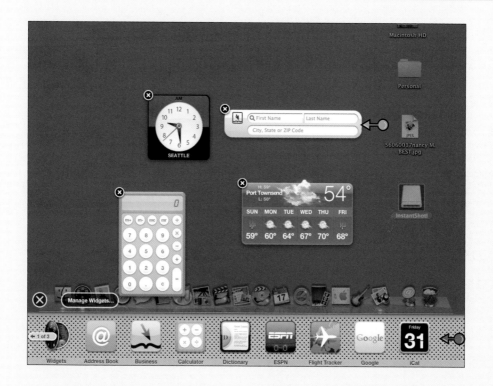

The Dashboard

The Dashboard allows you to display widgets. These useful little tools can include a calculator, clock, weather forecast, and calendar.

Widget Bar

You can customize the Dashboard to show any number of widgets from the Widget Bar.

Work with the Dock

The Dock is a strip of icons that provide shortcuts to a world of functionality. You can quickly launch items from the Dock. You can also customize the Dock to contain items that you use most often.

Whenever you launch an application, its icon appears on the Dock while it is active.

Work with the Dock

LAUNCH AN ITEM

① Move your mouse over an icon on the Dock.

● The icon name appears.

② Click the icon.

The application window appears.

③ Click **Close** ().

The application closes.

CUSTOMIZE THE DOCK

① Click **Finder** on the Dock.

② Click **Go** on the Finder menu bar.

③ Click **Applications**.

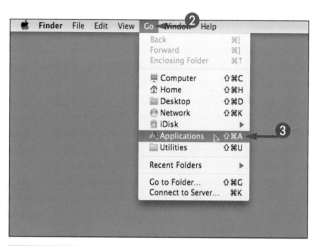

The Applications window appears.

④ Double-click an application that is not on the Dock.

The application opens and its icon appears on the Dock.

⑤ Press and hold Ctrl while you click the application icon.

⑥ Click **Keep in Dock**.

The item is now included in the Dock, even when it is inactive.

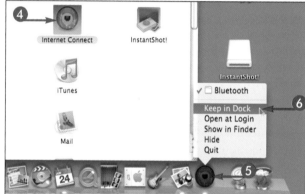

Can I remove an application from the Dock?

Yes. Press and hold Ctrl and then click the icon that you want to remove from the Dock. A small menu pops up, displaying a command to remove the item from the Dock. You can also remove an application from the Dock by simply clicking its icon and dragging it off of the Dock to the desktop.

What are the other commands that are available when I Ctrl-click a Dock item?

You can choose the **Show in Finder** command, that quickly opens Finder with that application already selected. You can also choose **Open at Login** to have the application open every time you login to your system.

Finder is similar to Windows Explorer, in that it is a window that contains lists of folders and devices on your computer. When you select a folder or device (such as your Macintosh hard drive) the contents are displayed in a main pane.

Explore the Finder

LOCATING AND OPENING ITEMS

1 Click **Finder**.

2 Click an item in the Sidebar to open it.

The contents of that item display.

***Note:** If you click an item with subfolders, you will need to click an arrow to display those subfolders.*

3 Double-click an item to open it.

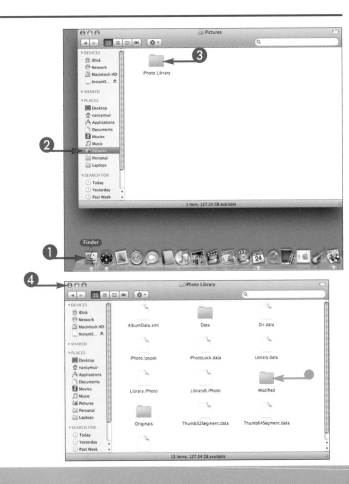

● Sub-folders display for the item that you opened.

You can double-click one of these items to open it.

4 Click ⊙.

The window closes.

CHANGE FINDER VIEWS

1 With Finder open, click a view button.

*Note: You can also click the **Options** menu, choose **View**, and then select a view from the submenu that appears.*

2 Click the **Options** button.

3 Click **Show View Options**.

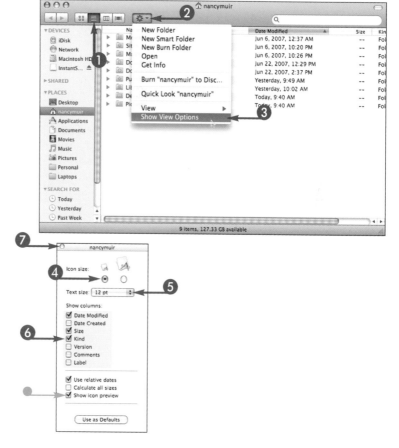

The Desktop dialog appears.

4 Click here to select the icon size you want to view (◯ changes to ◉).

5 Click here and select the text size you want.

6 Click the columns you want to display (☐ changes to ☑).

● Click other options to use settings such as showing icon previews (☐ changes to ☑).

7 Click .

Mac OS X applies your setting changes.

TIPS

The Size column in the Finder just contains two dashed lines. How can I get file sizes to display?

You can click the **Options** button and select **Show View Options**. In the pane that appears, click the **Calculate All Sizes** check box (☐ changes to ☑).

What does clicking the Use as Defaults button in the View Options dialog box do?

Once you have made changes to these settings, you can click the **Use as Defaults** button to restore all settings for the Finder view back to their default settings. This saves you from having to revert these changes one by one.

Work with the Keyboard and Trackpad

Your portable Mac includes some special keys that add functionality to the more compact keyboard. In addition, you can customize some options for the built-in trackpad mouse.

Use the Trackpad

Mac laptops use a trackpad-style mouse. This consists of a flat panel over which you move your finger to direct mouse actions, and a button area at the bottom that you tap to perform a clicking action. You can use System Preferences to modify the speeds for tracking and double-clicking when you use the trackpad.

Use Trackpad Gestures

You can modify your trackpad settings in System Preferences to use Gestures. Gestures allow you to set up the trackpad so that tapping the pad area, rather than the button area, performs a clicking action. If you select the Gestures clicking option, you can also enable dragging options that allow you to double-tap an item in the pad area to select it, and then drag the selected item around by moving your finger over the pad.

MacBook and MacBook Pro Function Keys

Because a laptop usually has a smaller keyboard, some actions are built into function key commands. On your MacBook or MacBook Pro, you have an Fn key that you can press along with another key to invoke an action, such as Fn+ 0 to enter a forward slash character (/). You can also press any of the numbered function keys along the top of the keyboard to perform different tasks. For example, pressing F1 or F2 controls screen brightness, F3 to F5 control speaker volume, and F12 ejects disks.

Customize the Keyboard

You can customize your keyboard shortcut settings through System Preferences. In the System Preferences window, you simply double-click a shortcut and then press the new keystroke combination that you want to use to invoke the shortcut. If you ever decide to go back to the original settings—for example, if another Mac user is using your laptop—then you can click the **Restore Defaults** button in the Keyboard & Mouse pane of System Preferences.

Exposé is a feature that helps you instantly control the arrangement of open windows on your Mac desktop to get rid of clutter.

Understanding Exposé

Exposé is always on and available to you. It operates through three function keys, which allow you to miniaturize and realign windows in a variety of ways. You can also use Exposé to scroll through currently open application windows.

Miniaturize and Realign All Windows

You can press the F9 key to miniaturize and arrange all open windows on your screen. Moving your mouse over a window displays its name. Pressing F10 shows the front-most application, with other open applications dimmed in the background. You can press Tab to scroll through the applications.

Hide All Windows

You can instantly hide all open windows by pressing F11. This moves open windows off to the far edges of the screen, allowing you to access other desktop items, such as folders and files.

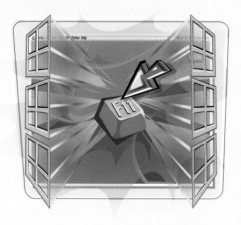

Assign Hot Corners

If you are not fond of function keys, you can also assign Exposé functions to any of the four corners of your screen, so that when you move your mouse over a corner, a function is invoked. You can set up these so-called hot corners using the System Preferences, Exposé, and Spaces pane.

Work with Widgets

Before Windows Vista had gadgets, Macs had widgets. These are small applications that provide handy items such as a clock, a calculator, or a display of the current weather information. You can display these widgets in the Dashboard, and choose which widgets you want to see.

Work with Widgets

OPEN THE DASHBOARD AND WIDGET BAR

① Click **Dashboard**.

② Move your mouse over a widget.

③ Click the information symbol (**i**).

Note: Some widgets, such as the calculator, do not have settings.

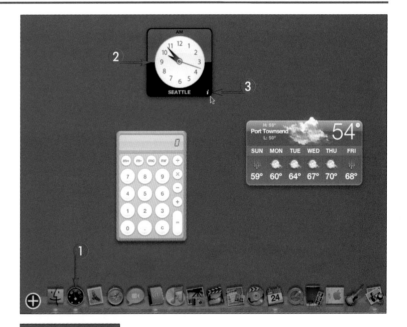

Settings appear for that widget.

④ Change the settings as needed.

⑤ Click **Done**.

The changes take effect.

ADD WIDGETS TO THE DASHBOARD

1 Click the plus sign (⊕).

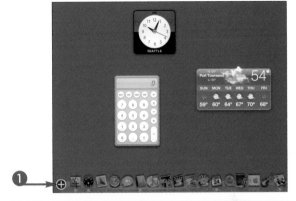

● The Widget Bar appears.

2 Click the arrows (◄ and ►) at either end to display more widgets.

3 Click and drag a widget onto the desktop.

Note: You can click anywhere on the desktop to hide the Widget Bar and Dashboard.

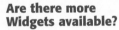

How do I remove a widget from the Dashboard?

When you click the plus sign (⊕) with the Dashboard displayed, it not only displays the Widget Bar but it also displays small X buttons on each widget on the Dashboard (see the fourth figure above). Click the button on the widget that you do not need to remove it from the Dashboard.

Are there more Widgets available?

Yes. Go to **www.apple.com/ downloads/ dashboard** and you will find a list of Top Widgets such as Wikipedia or Flapple, and a Widget Browser that lets you search for Widgets in a variety of categories.

Explore the Internet with Safari

Safari is the browser that is built into the Mac operating system. It offers familiar browser tools, such as bookmarks and the ability to view your browsing history.

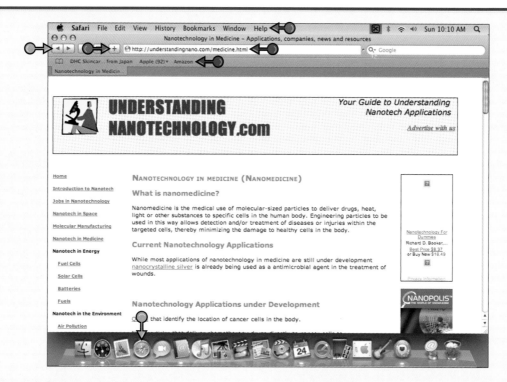

Safari Button
Click this button to open the Safari browser.

Safari Menus
Use the commands on these menus to change Safari settings, customize toolbars, edit text and modify text size, or view browsing history.

Address Bar
Enter the URL for the site you want to visit here, and press Enter.

Navigation Keys
Click the Show Next Page or Show Previous Page buttons to move among recently displayed Web pages.

Bookmark Bar
Bookmarked sites display on this bar.

Add a Bookmark
Click here to bookmark the currently displayed page.

When you work on a laptop, you can use power management to keep your computer working longer between battery charges.

Sleep Mode

Your laptop uses much less power in sleep mode. You can set up sleep modes to activate for both the computer screen and the computer processor.

Energy Saver Pane

In the System Preferences window, you will find an Energy Saver icon. Click it to display the Energy Saver pane. Here you can select settings to put your computer or screen to sleep when the computer has been inactive for a certain period of time. You can also set up your screen saver from this pane.

Energy-Saving Tips

You can be your most important energy-saving resource. Remember these tips. Turn off the Airport and Bluetooth wireless connection if there are no wireless networks nearby or you do not intend to use the Internet. Be sure the built-in iSight camera is turned off if you are not working with an application that requires it. Avoid working from DVDs or CDs, which require that the laptop motor spins and drains power. Instead, copy the files you need to your laptop and remove the disc. Finally, MacBooks contain a backlight in their keyboards that can be very helpful when working in dim lighting, but that consumes energy. Use the Backlight toggle key on your keyboard to turn it off.

Battery Settings

You can go through the Energy Saver pane in System Preferences (see the section "Energy Saver Pane" section earlier in this chapter) to change the battery optimization setting. The Better Battery Life setting will give you the longest battery life.

Exploring Windows Vista

The Windows Vista operating system is installed on most laptops on the market today. It enables you to run programs and manage files, and provides some useful mini-applications. Learning your way around the Windows environment is your first step to laptop productivity.

The Windows Vista desktop is what you see onscreen when you are not working in an application. It is from here that you access programs, files, and settings for Windows Vista.

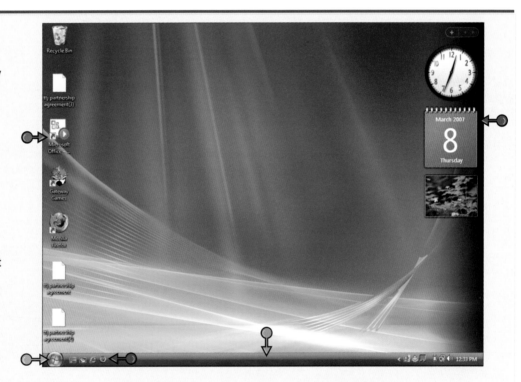

Start Menu Button

Click the Start button to display a menu of available programs, or to go to the Windows Help and Support area or the Control Panel.

Desktop Shortcuts

Rather than go through the Start menu, you can create a shortcut for a program or document and launch it by double-clicking the desktop shortcut icon.

Windows Vista Sidebar

New to Windows Vista, the Sidebar is where you can display various useful little programs, such as a clock, calculator, or stock market ticker.

Taskbar

The taskbar displays a button for each open application window that has been minimized (shrunk down to a button on the taskbar), as well as buttons to launch tools such as the system volume.

Quick Launch Bar

If you want convenient access to programs that you use frequently but do not want to use desktop shortcuts, you can place buttons for these programs on the Quick Launch bar and click the buttons to launch the programs.

The Start menu is where you can access and open installed software, useful accessory programs that are built into Windows Vista (such as Paint), and settings for Windows.

Access the Start Menu

① Click the **Start** button ().

Note: You can also press the **Start** key on your keyboard (with the Windows logo on it) to display the Start menu.

② Click **All Programs**.

All installed programs display in the left panel of the Start menu.

③ Click the **Accessories** folder.

You may have to use the scroll bar to locate this folder.

Windows Vista lists the accessory programs.

Add a Desktop Shortcut

Desktop shortcuts can provide a quick way to access your most commonly used programs or documents. Your laptop probably came with some shortcuts, such as the Recycle Bin and some pre-installed applications, but you can also add your own.

Add a Desktop Shortcut

① Click the **Start** button (🟦).

The Start menu opens.

② Click **All Programs**.

All installed programs display in the left panel of the Start menu.

③ Right-click the program for which you want to create a shortcut.

A menu appears.

④ Click **Send To**.

⑤ Click **Desktop (create shortcut)**.

● The shortcut appears on the desktop.

TIP

Sometimes I prefer a less cluttered look on the desktop. Is there an easy way to hide all desktop shortcuts from view?

Yes. Right-click the desktop and click **View** in the menu that appears. Click the **Show Desktop Icons** option to deselect it. To redisplay the icons, repeat this procedure.

Work with the Recycle Bin

The Recycle Bin is a desktop shortcut that accesses the folder where any deleted items are stored before Windows completely removes them. If you delete something and you want it back, you can look for it here. To save memory, you should also periodically empty the Recycle Bin.

Work with the Recycle Bin

RESTORE A DELETED ITEM

1 Double-click the **Recycle Bin** shortcut icon.

● The Recycle Bin folder opens in Windows Explorer.

2 Click an item to select it.

3 Click **Restore**.

The item is restored to the folder where it was stored when you deleted it.

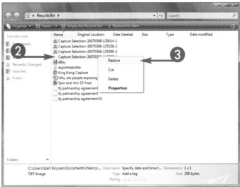

EMPTY THE RECYCLE BIN

① Right-click the **Recycle Bin** shortcut.

A shortcut menu appears.

② Click **Empty Recycle Bin**.

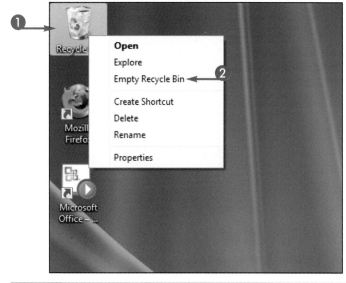

A confirmation dialog box appears.

③ Click **Yes**.

All items in the Recycle Bin are permanently deleted.

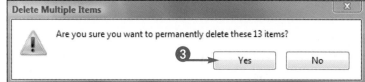

I cannot find the Recycle Bin. How can I display it?

Right-click the desktop and click **Personalize**. In the Personalize options, click the **Change Desktop Items** link on the left. In the dialog box that appears, click the **Recycle Bin** check box to select it, and then click **OK**. The desktop shortcut icon appears for the Recycle Bin.

Once I have emptied the Recycle Bin, can I be sure that my files are gone from my computer's hard drive?

No. Because hard drives use magnetic recording, they can contain residual data, even after you 'permanently' delete files. If you are selling or getting rid of your computer, you still run the risk of old files being restored by an ambitious hacker. Removing the hard drive may be your only completely secure option.

Adjust System Volume

The Windows Vista taskbar contains a shortcut for adjusting your system volume. You can also quickly mute your speakers by using this feature.

You can make more detailed settings to your system volume through the Hardware and Sound area of the Control Panel.

① Click the **Megaphone** icon on the taskbar.

The volume slider appears.

② Click and drag the slider (▯) to adjust the volume up or down.

③ Click the **Mute** button (◀●).

A red circle appears on the Mute button, to indicate that your speakers are muted. To restore sound, you can repeat Step **3**.

The Sidebar is a new feature in Windows Vista. It contains items called *gadgets* that perform useful functions, such as calculating numbers or displaying current news items.

Display and Close the Sidebar

1 Click the **Windows Sidebar** icon (▣) on the taskbar.

Note: *The Sidebar displays by default. If it is closed, the Sidebar icon should appear in the taskbar.*

2 Right-click anywhere on the Sidebar.

A shortcut menu appears.

3 Click **Close Sidebar**.

The Sidebar disappears from your screen.

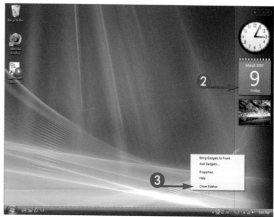

Work with Gadgets

Gadgets are the little programs that you can place on the Windows Vista Sidebar. These are very useful tools that can display updated online content such as stock quotes, or tools like a calculator or a tiny notepad.

Work with Gadgets

ADD A GADGET TO THE SIDEBAR

① With the Sidebar displayed, click the **Gadgets** button (▦).

Note: *To display the Sidebar, see the task "Display and Close the Sidebar."*

The Gadgets dialog box appears.

② Click and drag a gadget to the Sidebar.

The gadget appears on the Sidebar.

MOVE A GADGET TO THE DESKTOP

1 With the Sidebar displayed, move your mouse over a gadget.

● Small tool icons appear to the right of the gadget.

2 Click the **Move** tool (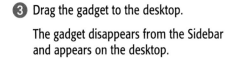)

3 Drag the gadget to the desktop.

The gadget disappears from the Sidebar and appears on the desktop.

TIP

I want to remove a gadget from the Sidebar. How do I do that?

Simply click the **Close** button, labeled with an *X*, to close the gadget. You can redisplay it by clicking the **Gadgets** button and then clicking and dragging the gadget from the Gadgets dialog box to the Sidebar.

continued

Once you have placed gadgets on your Windows sidebar, you can modify how some of them work. For example, if you display a clock gadget, you can change your time zone or specify whether to display a second hand.

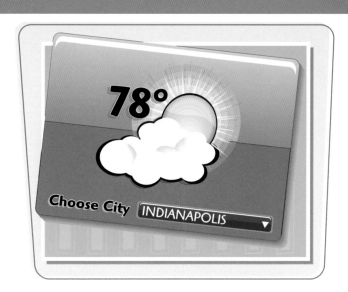

Work with Gadgets *(continued)*

MODIFY GADGET SETTINGS

① With the Sidebar displayed, move your mouse over a gadget.

Note: *To display the Windows Sidebar, see the task "Display and Close the Sidebar."*

● Small tool icons appear to the right of the gadget.

② Click the wrench-shaped tool.

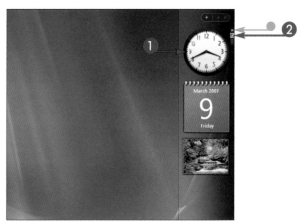

A pop-up window appears with gadget settings.

Note: *Some tools have no settings, and therefore no wrench icon appears.*

③ Make the appropriate settings for that gadget.

④ Click **OK** to save the settings.

GET MORE GADGETS ONLINE

1 With the Sidebar displayed, click the **Gadgets** button (■).

The Gadgets dialog box appears.

2 Click **Get more gadgets online**.

Your Web browser opens, displaying the Personalize Windows Vista Sidebar Web page.

● You can click the categories to look for specific gadgets.

3 When you find the gadget you want, click the Download button.

Note: Instructions may appear to help you complete the download.

The gadget is now available in the Gadgets dialog box to add to your Sidebar.

TIP

I have a lot of gadgets in my collection. How can I easily find the one I want?

You can use the Search feature in the Gadgets dialog box. Just type in a keyword, and press Enter.

Work with Windows Explorer

Windows Explorer is a Windows Vista feature that you can use to locate various files and folders that you have saved on your computer.

① Right-click the **Start** button (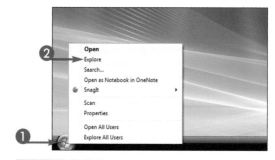).

A shortcut menu appears.

② Click **Explore**.

The Windows Explorer window appears.

③ Click a folder.

4 If necessary, click a series of folders to locate the file that you want to open.

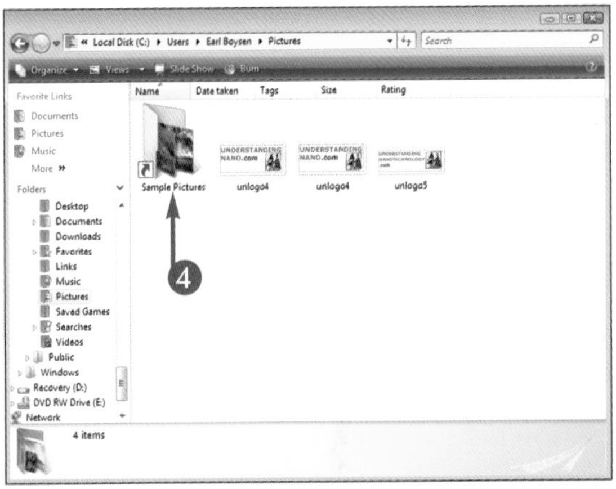

5 Double-click the file.

The contents of the file display in the Explorer window.

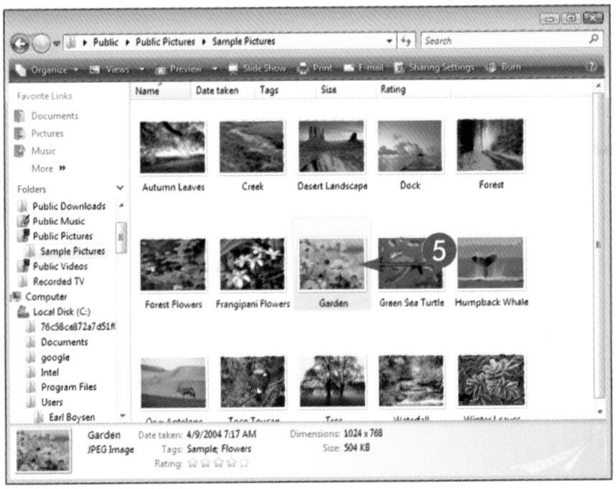

TIPS

I use files from the Documents folder all the time. Is there a quick way to open it?

Yes. The Start menu lists several commonly used folders, including Documents, Pictures, and Music. Just click the **Start** button and then click **Documents** to open the Documents folder.

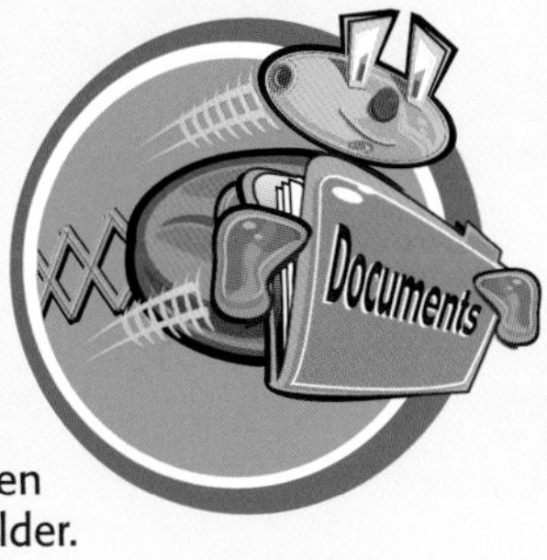

I cannot remember a filename, but I know I worked on it yesterday. Is there a way to see what date a file was last saved in Windows Explorer?

Yes. With Windows Explorer open, click the **Views** button and then click **Details**. The Details view lists information about each folder and file, including the date it was last modified.

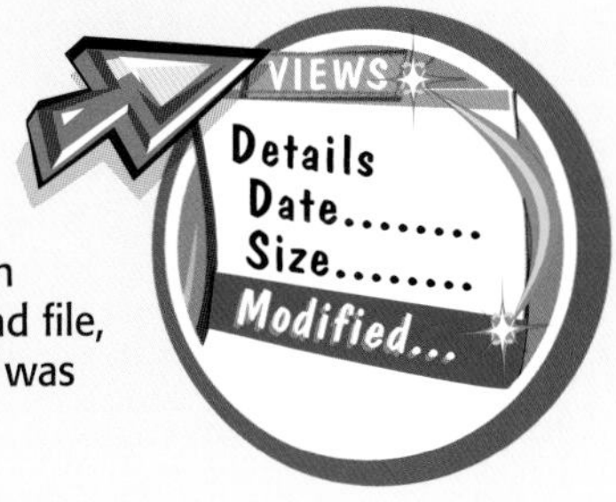

Change the Screen Resolution

Your screen resolution setting controls the crispness of the image on your monitor. A higher resolution results in more pixels per inch, making the screen image smaller and crisper. A lower resolution causes items to appear larger, but less clearly defined on your screen.

Change the Screen Resolution

① Right-click the Windows Vista desktop.

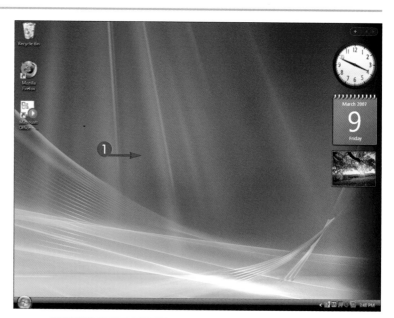

A shortcut menu appears.

② Click **Personalize**.

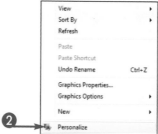

View	▶
Sort By	▶
Refresh	
Paste	
Paste Shortcut	
Undo Rename	Ctrl+Z
Graphics Properties...	
Graphics Options	▶
New	▶
Personalize	

The Personalize appearance and sounds options appear.

③ Click **Display Settings**.

The Display Settings dialog box appears.

④ Click and drag the **Resolution** slider () to change the resolution.

⑤ Click **Apply** to apply the resolution setting.

⑥ Click **OK** to close the dialog box.

TIP

Which resolution setting will allow me to see more of my document onscreen at one time?

A higher resolution allows more of your document to fit on your screen. Remember, you can also use the View tools in individual software applications to display your document in a larger or smaller view.

Change the Desktop Background

The background on your desktop can be a simple solid color. However, if you want a little more variety, you can display a picture that comes with Windows Vista, or a picture of your own that you have saved to your computer.

1 Right-click the desktop.

A shortcut menu appears.

2 Click **Personalize**.

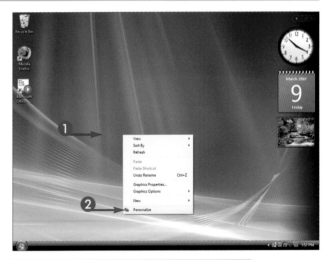

The Personalize appearance and sounds options appear.

3 Click **Desktop Background**.

4 Click the **Picture Location** ⊡ and select a category of desktop background options.

5 Click the image you want to use.

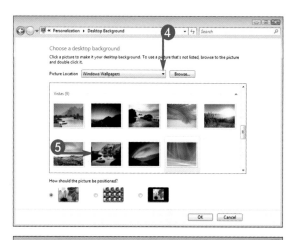

6 Click a positioning option for the image (◯ changes to ◉):

Fit to Screen stretches a single copy of the image across the screen.

Tile displays several copies of the image across the desktop.

Center centers a single image against a colored background.

7 Click **OK**.

Windows Vista applies the settings.

I applied a desktop theme and my background changed. Why?

A desktop theme contains a background setting, as well as other settings such as a color scheme. If you apply a desktop theme, then it overrides whatever background you have selected.

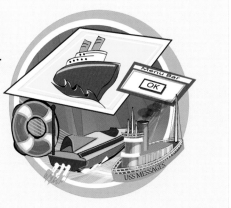

Get Help

The Windows Vista Help and Support feature allows you to look through various help topics and sub-topics. If you are connected to the Internet, Windows Vista also searches for the latest help information in the Microsoft Knowledge database.

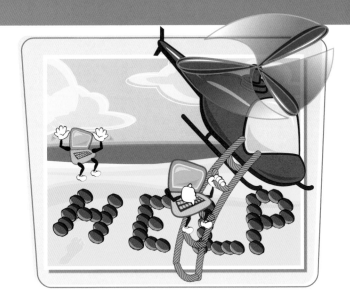

Get Help

EXPLORE THE HELP TABLE OF CONTENTS

1. Click **Start** ( ).

2. Click **Help and Support**.

   The Windows Help and Support window appears.

3. Click **Table of Contents**.

   A list of major topics is displayed.

4. Click any topic.

   A set of sub-topic folders and/or search results indicated by a question mark ( ). displays.

5. If necessary, click a sub-topic results.

   The information displays.

Note: *You may have to click several levels of sub-topics to access the topic information.*

SEARCH FOR HELP

1 Type in a search term.

2 Click **Search Help** ().

The search results display.

3 Click a link to display the topic.

Windows displays the topic you selected.

TIP

What are the words in green within topic information?

In some topics, terms that include a definition appear in green. Click these terms to display their definition. Click anywhere outside of the definition window to close it.

Ask for Remote Assistance

You can use the Remote Assistance feature in Windows Vista Help to invite a friend to help you. Using this feature, someone else can take over your computer to view and fix a problem — with your permission.

① Click **Start** (⊞).

② Click **Help and Support.**

The Windows Help and Support window appears.

③ Click the **Windows Remote Assistance** link.

The Windows Remote Assistance dialog box appears.

④ Click **Invite Someone You Trust to Help You**.

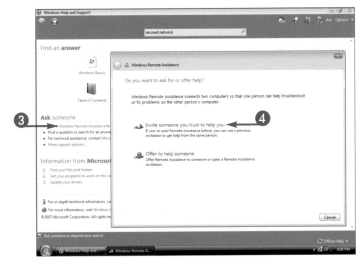

Windows asks you how to contact your helper.

⑤ Click **Use e-mail to send an invitation**.

● Clicking **Save this invitation as a file** enables you to send the file as an attachment.

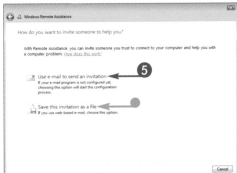

Windows asks you for a password for connecting to your computer.

6 Type in a password.

7 Type the password again.

8 Click **Next**.

A blank e-mail form opens in your default e-mail program.

Note: If you have not set up an e-mail account on your laptop, a series of dialog boxes appear for you to fill out.

9 Fill out the e-mail address, and add to or edit the message if you want.

10 Click **Send**.

When a connection is made, you can use the tools in the Windows Remote Assistance window to change settings; chat with your friend; send a file; or pause, cancel, or stop sharing your computer.

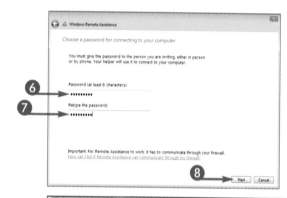

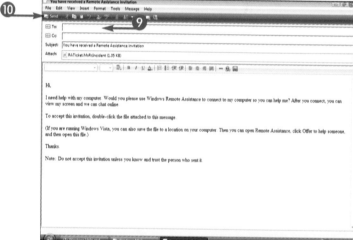

I cannot seem to make a Remote Assistance connection. Why not?

You probably have to enable the feature. Click **Start**, click **Control Panel**, click **System and Maintenance**, click **System**, and then click **Remote Settings**. On the Remote tab of the dialog box that appears, select the **Allow Remote Assistance Connections to this Computer** check box (changes to). Click **OK**, and you should be able to use the feature.

File Management Basics

Windows Vista and the Macintosh OS use a file and folder system to organize your documents — a metaphor for the manila files and hanging folders that you find for organizing paper documents in most offices. Understanding how to work with files and folders helps you to be much more efficient.

Create a New Folder

Windows comes with some folders already created, such as Documents, Pictures, and Music. You can also create additional folders for specific projects, clients, or interests.

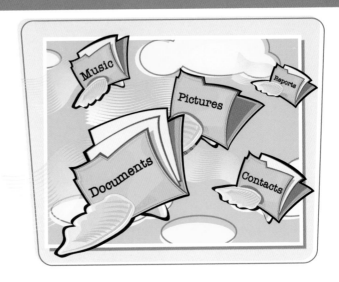

Create a New Folder

① Right-click **Start** (⊞).

② Click **Explore**.

Windows Explorer appears.

③ Click **Organize**.

④ Click **New Folder**.

A new folder appears with its name highlighted for editing.

⑤ Type a folder name.

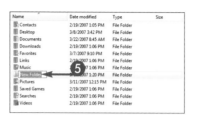

⑥ Press **Enter**.

⑦ Click **Close** (✕) to close Windows Explorer.

Copy a File

You may want to keep a copy of a file in two different folders. For example, you might want to have a copy of a letter to your client in both the general client folder and in a project folder.

Copy a File

① Right-click .

② Click **Explore**.

Windows Explorer appears.

③ Click any folder in the left panel to open its contents.

Note: You may have to click on a series of folders and sub-folders to locate the file you want.

④ Right-click the file you want to copy.

⑤ Click **Copy**.

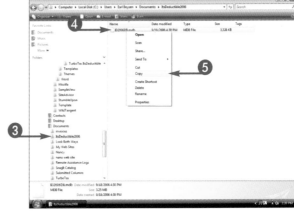

⑥ Double-click the folder into which you want to place the copied file.

● You can use the **Folders** list on the left side of the Explorer window to find a file.

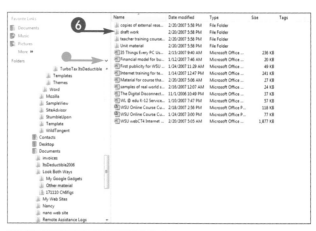

⑦ Right-click the Explorer window.

⑧ Click **Paste**.

The copy of the file appears listed in the folder contents.

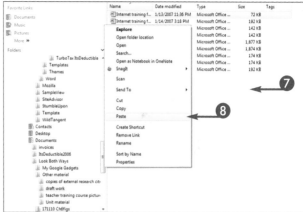

TIP

Is there any other way to copy a file from one folder to another?
Yes. You can click and drag a file between two open Explorer windows. Click the file and hold down Ctrl. When you drag the file to the other folder, a copy is placed there.

Move
a File

After you save a file in one folder, you may decide to move it into another folder, perhaps when you are archiving old documents or reorganizing your files.

Move a File

1 Right-click .

2 Click **Explore**.

Windows Explorer appears.

3 Click a folder in the left pane to display its contents.

Note: *You may have to click on a folder and sub-folders to locate the file you need.*

Right-click the file you want to move.

4 Click **Cut**.

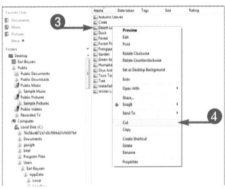

⑤ Double-click the folder in which you want to place the file.

● You can use the Folders list on the left side of the Explorer window to find a file.

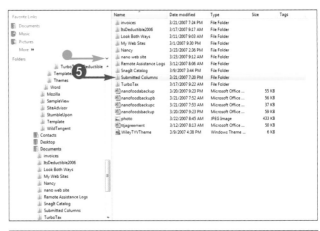

⑥ Right-click the Explorer window.

⑦ Click **Paste**.

The file appears listed in the folder contents.

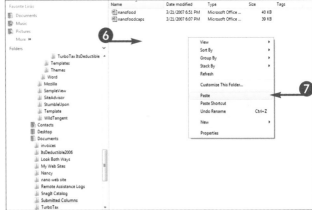

Is there a click-and-drag method for moving files?

Yes. Open two Explorer windows (right-click 🖼 and choose **Explore** two times in a row). Click and drag the file you want to move, but without holding down **Ctrl** as you do to copy a file. The file is removed from one folder and placed in another.

I cut a file, but before I could paste it, I was called away from the computer. When I came back, it seemed to be gone. Is there a way to retrieve it?

Yes. When you cut the file, it was placed in the Recycle Bin folder. Go to your desktop and open the Recycle Bin folder. Click the file and then click **Restore this Item**.

If your project name changes or you realize that your filename has a typo or resembles another name too closely, you may want to rename the file.

You cannot have two files in the same folder with the same name, but you can have two files with the same name in different folders. Try to avoid naming two files with the same name to avoid confusion.

Rename a File

① Right-click .

② Click **Explore**.

Windows Explorer appears.

③ Right-click the file.

④ Click **Rename**.

Windows highlights the filename for editing.

⑤ Type a new name.

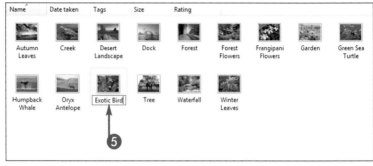

⑥ Press Enter.

● The file appears with its new name.

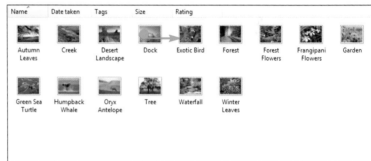

TIP

I renamed a file and now I cannot remember the new name. How can I find it?

You can easily search for files and folders by using a variety of criteria, such as the last time it was modified or by words contained in the document. See the task "Search for Files and Folders" later in this chapter.

Compress Files

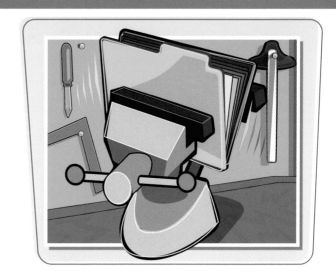

Compressing files essentially squeezes them down to a smaller size. You can then extract the files at a later time to work with them again.

Compress Files

1 Right-click .

2 Click **Explore**.

Windows Explorer appears.

3 Right-click a file.

4 Click **Send to**.

5 Click **Compressed (zipped) Folder**.

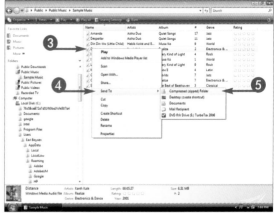

A dialog box appears, displaying the
progress of the compression operation.

● A new folder appears, with its name
highlighted for editing.

⑥ Type a new name for the file.

⑦ Press Enter.

The new name is saved for the
compressed file.

Name	Artists	Album	#	Genre	Rating
Amanda	Aisha Duo	Quiet Songs	17	Jazz	
Despertar	Aisha Duo	Quiet Songs	11	Jazz	
Din Din Wo (Little Child)	Habib Koité and B...	Muso Ko	9	World	
Distance	Karsh Kale	Realize	2	Electronica & ...	
Distance					
I Guess You're Right	The Posies	Every Kind of Light	4	Rock	
I Ka Barra (Your Work)	Habib Koité and B...	Muso Ko	1	World	
Love Comes	The Posies	Every Kind of Light	9	Rock	
Muita Bobeira	Luciana Souza; Ro...	Duos II	4	Latin	
OAM's Blues	Aaron Goldberg	Worlds	7	Jazz	
One Step Beyond	Karsh Kale	Realize	7	Electronica & ...	
Symphony No. 3 in E-f...	Nicolaus Esterhaz...	The Best of Beethoven	3	Classical	

I want to compress several files. Can I do that?

Yes. To compress several files together, click one file and then press Shift and select contiguous files, or Ctrl-click non-contiguous files before you right-click.

I have a new computer with a huge hard drive. What is the benefit of compressing a file or folder?

It is true that a compressed file or folder takes up less space on your computer. If that is not of concern to you, you may find other situations in which you want to compress files. For example, you may want to save space on a storage medium such as a CD. Also, if you are attaching a file or folder to an e-mail, you need to keep the attachment size as small as possible so that it can go through.

Work with File Formats

Files can be saved in a variety of formats recognizable to certain programs. Understanding file formats helps you to understand how to find and open files easily.

File Format Overview

Most files are saved by default in the format of the program that is used to create them. Because this so-called "native" format is often proprietary, other programs may or may not be able to open these files.. However, many programs today can open files saved in a variety of formats, for example, text files to be opened by almost any word processing application. There are also formats, such as Adobe PDF, that can be read by any program; these require a reader that can usually be downloaded for free.

Text Formats

When you save a text file, you can save it in the format of the program you are working in, such as Word (DOC) or WordPerfect (WKB). You can also save a text file in rich text format (RTF), which is a format that many programs can open and that retains most of your text formatting. Finally, saving a file using the text format (TXT) saves the text, but with no formatting.

Image Formats

Digital image files can be saved in several formats, many of which can be inserted into most documents. Each of those formats has certain characteristics. For example, JPEG is a format that compresses a graphics file to be smaller than some other formats. GIF format is often used for low resolution graphics files that are viewed online and that require image compression. Other common graphics file formats include TIFF, BMP, and PNG.

Web Formats

If you want to post documents on the Web, you can save to Web formats such as HTML, XML, or MHTML. When posted to the Internet, these formats can be read by Web browsers.

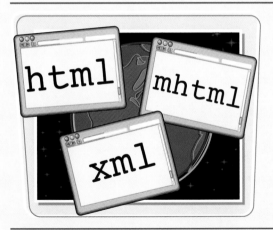

Macintosh File Formats

Macintosh program files usually cannot be opened by Windows programs, and vice-versa. However, you can save files from either type of program in another format that can be recognized by the other operating system. You can also set up a Macintosh to run the Windows operating system in addition to the Macintosh operating system. This requires that you purchase a software product called Boot Camp from Apple.

After creating a file — such as a document where you enter text or insert images — you have to save the file before closing it if you want to use it again.

You can save a file to your hard drive, or to media such as a CD or DVD.

Save Files

1 With an application and new document open, click **File**.

2 Click **Save**.

You can also press **Ctrl** + **S** or click a **Save** button in most software programs.

Note: If you have already saved the file, this is all you have to do to save recent changes. If this is the first time you have saved the file, continue with the following steps.

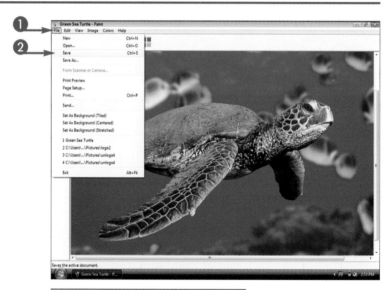

3 Click the folder to which you want to save the file.

You may need to click the a folder in the list in the left pane to locate the folder or drive where you want to save the file.

④ Click here and type a name for the document.

⑤ Click **Save**.

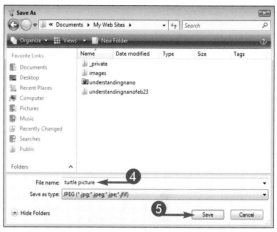

● The filename appears in the title bar.

TIP

How do I save a file in a different format?

In the Save As dialog box, use the Save as Type drop-down list to select the format you want to save to before clicking **Save**.

Back Up Files

It is important to save your files to media such as a CD or DVD in order to keep a backup copy. To help you, Windows Vista provides a feature to guide you through backing up your computer files.

① Click .

② Click **Control Panel**.

The Control Panel window appears.

③ Click **Back up your computer**.

Windows presents options for backing up and restoring files.

④ Click **Back up files**.

Note: Windows does not run the backup procedure for laptops if they are running on battery power.

The Back Up Files dialog box appears.

⑤ Click to select the backup destination.

You can choose to back up to media such as a flash drive, or to a location on a network.

⑥ Click **Next**.

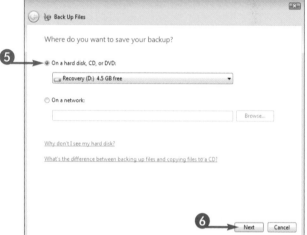

TIP

I noticed that there is an option to back up your computer. Why would I do that?

When you first get your computer, it is a good idea to create a set of backup discs for it. Then, if you experience a serious problem and have to restore your computer to its original settings, you can use those discs to do so.

continued

Back Up Files
(continued)

The Windows Backup feature allows you to choose a specific time to back up files automatically; for example, you can back up your files weekly on Fridays at 10 pm. This ensures that your computer periodically saves all your important files, even if you forget to.

7 Click to select the types of files that you want to back up (☐ changes to ☑).

8 Click **Next.**

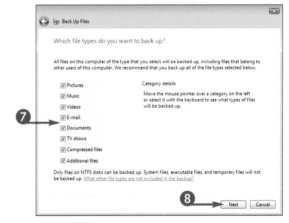

9 Click ▾ to set the timing of the backup:

● **How often** sets the time increment.

● **What day** specifies the day to back up.

● **What time** sets the time of day to begin the backup.

10 Click **Save settings and start backup**.

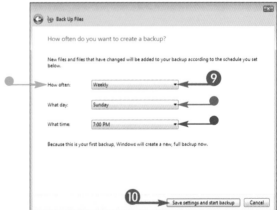

A progress window appears.

● If you want to halt the backup you can click the **Stop Backup** button at any time.

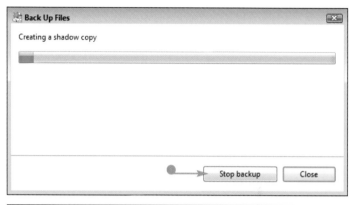

⑪ When the backup is complete a confirmation message appears; click Close.

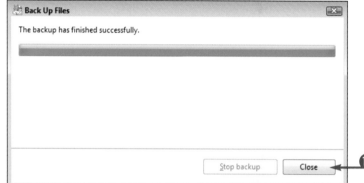

TIPS

Can I use the Backup procedure to save my system files?

No. System files, executable files (such as application installation files), and temporary files are not backed up using the Backup procedure. You would have to save copies of these files manually onto a storage media such as a CD or DVD. Another option is to create a System Restore point through the System and Maintenance options in the Control Panel that saves your system files as they are at a certain point in time.

I have Windows Vista Home Basic and I do not see a way to set up regular backups. What is the problem?

That version of Windows Vista does not allow you to set up periodic backups of your files. However the operating system will remind you to perform a backup periodically.

Delete Files

When you no longer need a file on your hard drive, you may want to delete it to keep your computer from becoming cluttered, or to save memory. You can delete single files or entire folders.

Delete Files

1 Right-click .

2 Click **Explore**.

Windows Explorer appears.

3 Click a folder in the left pane to locate the file or sub-folder that you want to delete.

4 Right-click the file or folder.

A shortcut menu appears.

5 Click **Delete.**

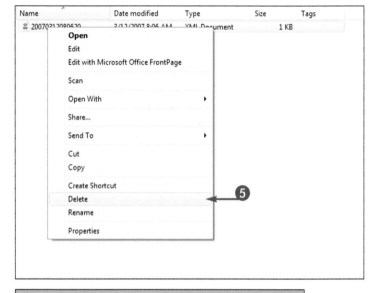

A confirmation dialog box appears.

6 Click **Yes**.

Windows moves the file to your Recycle Bin folder.

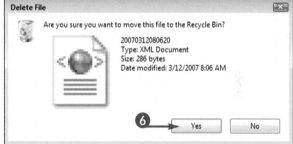

 TIP

What do I do if I delete a file and then decide I want it back?

Your Recycle Bin settings dictate a maximum size for the bin. When it is exceeded, Windows will permanently delete some files to make room for new deletions. So, for a time, your file is held in the Recycle Bin folder. Go to your desktop and double-click the **Recycle Bin** shortcut icon. Look in the list of items to find the file you want, select it, and then click the **Restore this Item** button.

Burn Files to a CD/DVD

You may want to copy files to storage media from time to time to keep a backup copy or to share large files like PowerPoint presentations with others.

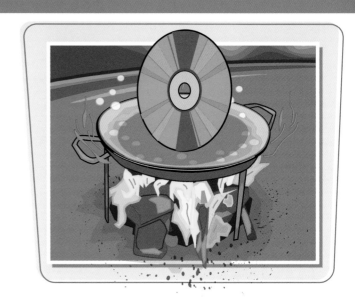

① Right-click .

② Click **Explore**.

Windows Explorer appears.

③ Right-click a file or folder.

If you want to burn multiple files, hold down Shift while clicking contiguous files, or hold down Ctrl while clicking non-contiguous files.

④ Click **Send to.**

⑤ Click the drive containing the storage media.

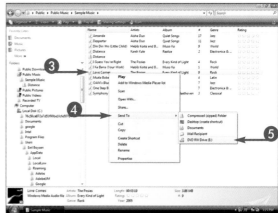

The Burn a Disc dialog box appears.

6 Type in a disc title.

7 Click **Next**.

8 Click the message that appears above the taskbar, indicating you have files to burn.

9 Click **Burn to disc**.

In the dialog box that appears, follow the directions in order to complete burning the files to disc.

 TIPS

Is there a way to quickly copy a file or folder that I saved to a DVD to my Documents folder?

Yes. Using Windows Explorer, right-click the item and choose the **Sent to** menu; however, this time, click **Documents** rather than a drive to send a copy from the DVD to your Documents folder.

What is the difference between the Burn a Disc format options?

The Live File System option is the default, and burns files to the disc immediately. The Mastered format stores files in a temporary staging area, ready for you to burn them to a disc at a later time. With the Mastered disc format you are also not allowed to delete files to make room for the new data. Mastered disc format is most useful on older computers or with CD or DVD players.

Search for Files and Folders

Sometimes you forget the name of a file or where you stored it in your folders. In that case, it is useful to be able to search for files or folders by a variety of criteria.

Windows offers both a simple and advanced search feature that allows you to search by criteria such as author, date created, or file size.

Search for Files and Folders

① Click ⬛.

② Click **Search**.

The Search Results window appears.

③ Type a search term in the Search field.

④ Press **Enter**.

A list of matching files displays.

5 Click **Advanced Search.**

Additional search criteria appear.

6 Click ▾ to choose Location, Date, or Size.

7 Type identifying information in the Name, Tags, or Authors fields.

*Note: Sometimes, files are set as hidden by users. If you want to search for hidden or system files, click the **Include non-indexed, hidden, and system files** check box in the Advanced Search window (changes to ✓).*

8 Click **Search**.

The search results display.

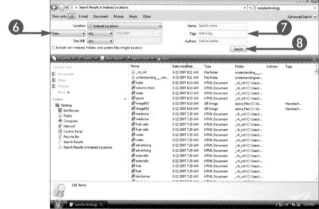

My search returned a list of files, but I would like to quickly identify the last file that I used. Can I do that?

Yes. You can use the Date setting in the advanced search window to do this, but you can also simply click the **Date** column heading in the search results to quickly organize the results by date.

Search by Date

Open Recently Used Files

If the file you need is one that you worked on recently, another quick way to locate it is to look for recently used files.

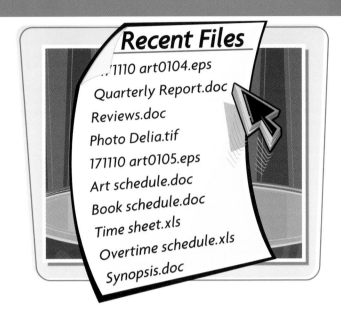

Recent Files

1110 art0104.eps
Quarterly Report.doc
Reviews.doc
Photo Delia.tif
171110 art0105.eps
Art schedule.doc
Book schedule.doc
Time sheet.xls
Overtime schedule.xls
Synopsis.doc

Open Recently Used Files

USE THE RECENT ITEMS FOLDER

① Click .

② Click **Recent Items**.

A list of files appears.

③ Click the item you want to open.

The file opens in the program that is associated with it.

FIND RECENTLY OPENED FILES IN AN APPLICATION

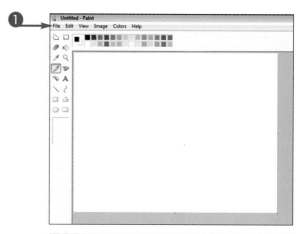

1 In an open application, click **File**.

*Note: In Office 2007 applications, click the **Office** button (⊞) to open the File menu.*

2 Click a file in the list of recently opened files.

The file opens in the application window.

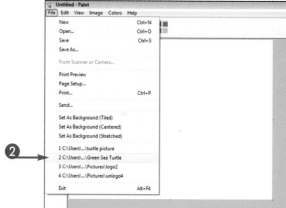

TIPS

Can I clear out the recently used files in the Start (⊞) menu?

Yes. You might want to do this if you do not want others to see the files you have been working on. Click ⊞ and then right-click **Recent Items**. Then click **Clear Recent Items List**.

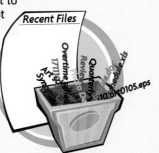

My computer opens word processor documents in Microsoft Word, but I would rather open them in Corel WordPerfect. Is there a way to set this up?

Yes. You can associate files with a particular program. Open Windows Explorer, click a file of the type you want, and click the **Open** button and click **Choose Default Program**. Click the **Browse** button and locate the program you want to use, and click **OK**.

Software Basics

Several software *applications* (also called *programs*) come pre-installed on your laptop, and you can install others as you need them. You should master a few basic skills to become comfortable with the look and feel of common software elements. This chapter explores both traditional Windows-based software and some of the new tools in Microsoft Office 2007. See Chapter 5 for more about Apple computers and software.

Install a Program

Whether you want to upgrade an existing program to a new version, or install a new piece of software, there are simple procedures that you can follow.

In many cases, simply inserting a CD-ROM or DVD causes a window to appear with software-specific instructions for installation.

Install a Program

INSTALL FROM A CD-ROM OR DVD

① Insert the CD-ROM or DVD into the appropriate drive.

The AutoPlay dialog box appears.

② Click the **Run** option.

If instructions appear to install the program, follow them. If the contents of the disc appear in a Windows Explorer window, proceed to Step **3**.

③ Double-click the **Setup.exe** file

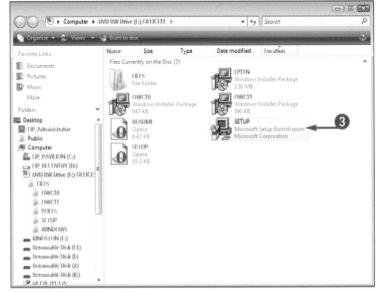

INSTALL FROM A DOWNLOADED FILE

1 Download the installation file from the software manufacturer's or software distributor's Web site.

This usually involves clicking a **Download** button or link.

2 In the dialog box that appears, click **Run**.

If you use a Macintosh computer, after you download a file, double-click the file in the Download Manager window.

A progress window appears.

3 Follow the instructions to install the program.

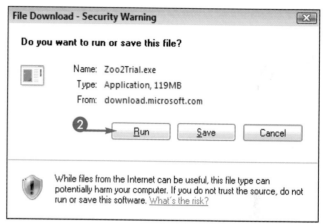

File Download - Security Warning

Do you want to run or save this file?

Name: Zoo2Trial.exe
Type: Application, 119MB
From: download.microsoft.com

2 → Run   Save   Cancel

While files from the Internet can be useful, this file type can potentially harm your computer. If you do not trust the source, do not run or save this software. What's the risk?

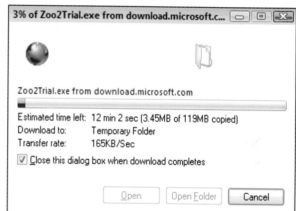

3% of Zoo2Trial.exe from download.microsoft.c...

Zoo2Trial.exe from download.microsoft.com

Estimated time left: 12 min 2 sec (3.45MB of 119MB copied)
Download to: Temporary Folder
Transfer rate: 165KB/Sec

☑ Close this dialog box when download completes

Open   Open Folder   Cancel

TIPS

I have Windows XP. What should I consider when installing programs with that operating system?

Windows XP and previous versions of Windows have an Add a Program command in the Control Panel. You can use that command, but most software today comes with its own installation program. As a result, even if you are running Windows XP, all you need to do is insert the disc in the appropriate drive and follow the directions.

I have a Mac and when I install software I am asked for a name and password. What is this?

These are the name and password you specified when you set up your Mac operating system. If you have more than one user account, make sure you use the name and password for that account.

Open a Program

Before you can work on a document, you have to launch the program that allows you to create and work in that kind of document. For example, you can use Microsoft Word to create a letter, or Adobe Photoshop to work with photos.

Open a Program

1 Click **Start** (⊞).

Note: *If the program that you need is listed in the first Start menu, click it and skip the remaining steps in this task.*

2 Click **All Programs**.

A list of programs appears.

3 Click the program or program folder you want to use.

The program opens and Windows Vista adds an item to the taskbar for the program.

Switch between Programs

If you have more than one program running simultaneously, such as a Web browser and a word processing application, you can switch between them whenever you want.

Switch between Programs

1 Click an open application on the taskbar.

Note: You can also press Alt + Tab and select the program from the window that appears

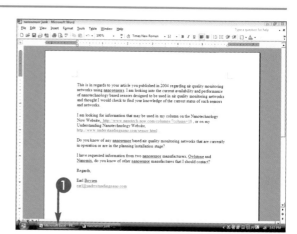

The program window appears.

Open a Document

When you or another user create and save a document, you can open and work on it again in the program in which it was created.

Open a Document

1 Launch the program in which you created the document.

2 Click **File**.

If you are working in a Microsoft Office 2007 application, click the **Office** button (📷).

3 Click **Open**.

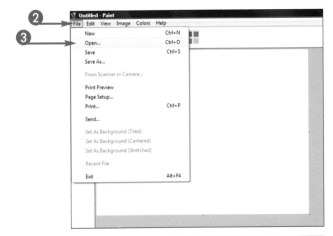

4 In the dialog box that appears, click the folder that contains the file you want to open.

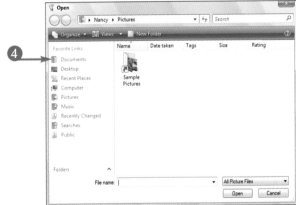

⑤ Double-click a subfolder to display its contents.

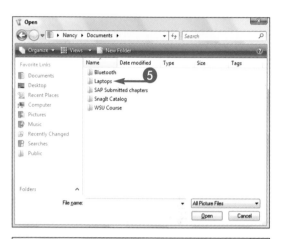

⑥ Click the document you want to open.

⑦ Click **Open**.

The document opens in the program window.

Note: You can use the Favorite Links list on the left side of the dialog box to find a file.

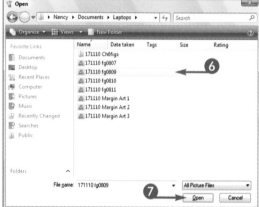

 TIPS

When I try to open a document, I get a message that no program is available. What does this mean?

This means that whatever program was used to create the document is not installed on the computer on which you are working. With Windows Vista, you are offered the option of going online to find a program. If the required program is free for download, such as a reader program, you can simply download and install it; if the program is a paid product, you will have to either install a trial version or buy the software to open and work on the document.

Is there a quicker way to open the document I last worked on?

Yes. If you open the Windows Start menu by clicking, you can click **Recent Items** and a list of files you worked on most recently appears. Most software programs also include a list of recently used files in their File menu (or whatever menu they offer to open a file).

Explore a Program Window

Most Windows-based software has similar elements that you can use to work with documents.

Toolbar
The toolbar contains buttons that you click to access common commands and options. Some buttons initiate a command, while others display lists or dialog boxes from which you can choose commands.

Menu Bar
The menu bar consists of drop-down menus and submenus that you can use to access commonly used commands. These commands may initiate an action or open a dialog box.

Minimize/Restore/Close Buttons
Click these buttons to reduce the size of the program window, restore the reduced window to fill the entire screen, or close the program.

Document Area
This is the central area of a program that you use to create documents. It is where you enter and edit text and place images that make up the document contents.

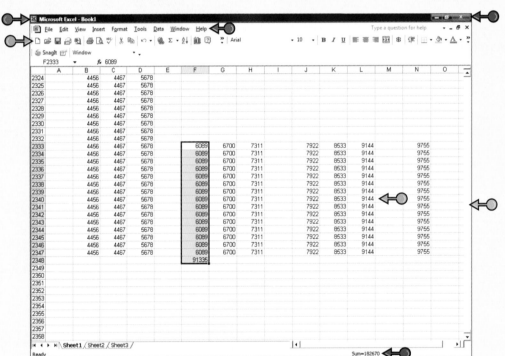

Status Bar
The status bar provides information about the current status of the program or document. For example, it might indicate the current page number in a document, or the current calculation in a spreadsheet. Office 2007 applications also offer tools on the status bar for changing views and zooming in or out.

Title Bar
The title bar contains the name of the currently open document and program. If the program window is reduced, you can move the program window by clicking and dragging the title bar.

Scroll bar
The scroll bar is useful for navigating through the pages of a document. The vertical scroll bar along the right side allows you to scroll up or down, while the horizontal scroll bar along the bottom of your screen allows you to scroll from side to side.

Select a Command from a Menu

Menus are used in many Windows-based programs. They offer a list of commands that you can choose from to perform different actions.

A command on a menu may initiate an action, display a submenu, or open a dialog box.

RUN COMMANDS

❶ Click a menu heading.

The drop-down menu appears.

Note: *You can also display a menu by pressing* **Alt** *and pressing the underlined letter in the menu name.*

❷ Click a command.

The program runs the command.

If clicking the command displays a submenu, you can move your cursor over to the submenu and click the command you want.

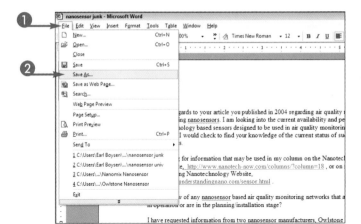

TOGGLE COMMANDS ON AND OFF

❶ Click a menu heading.

The program displays the menu, with check marks indicating the commands that are activated.

❷ Click the command.

If the menu displays a sub-menu, you can move your mouse over the submenu and click the commands you want to toggle on or off.

Note: *When you click a toggle command, the program either turns the feature on (✓) or off.*

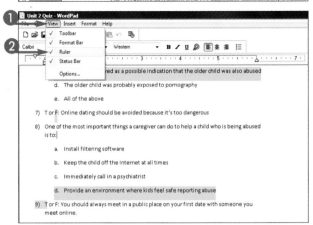

Select a Command from a Toolbar

Toolbars use a more graphical approach to choosing commands. They contain groups of buttons that you click to access commonly used features.

RUN A COMMAND USING A TOOL BUTTON

1 Click a tool button.

Note: *Some toolbar buttons stay activated after you click them, which means that they toggle a function on and off. You can click the button again to turn the feature off.*

The program runs the command or displays a dialog box, or a list of choices such as font sizes drops down; if you see a list, go to the next step.

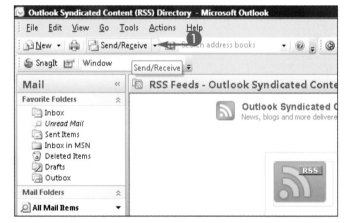

2 Click the command.

The program runs the command.

Note: *For more about using dialog boxes, see the task "Selecting Options in Dialog Boxes."*

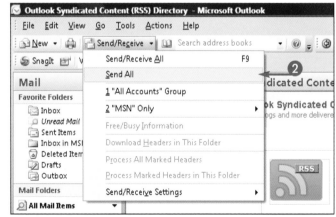

The Office 2007 program window offers a new look with many new tools for getting your work done. The Ribbon replaces toolbars and menus in previous editions of Office programs. Galleries of options allow you to preview results of choices before you apply them. Contextual tools appear when and where you need them.

Ribbon
Displays tabs that provide access to many tools that used to be embedded in dialog boxes.

Ribbon Group
Tools on the Ribbon are organized into groups by their type of function.

Dialog Box Launcher
For groups with additional functionality, click this to open a dialog box.

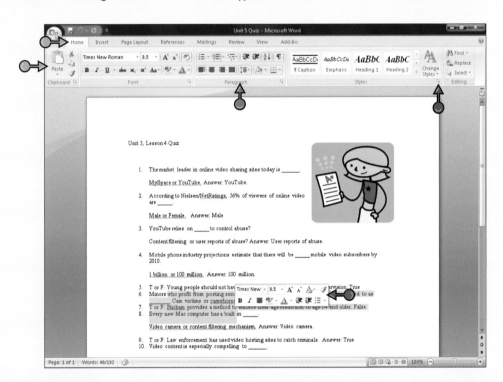

Ribbon Tabs
Display a different set of tools by clicking the appropriate Ribbon tab.

MiniBar
When you select text, this floating set of formatting tools appears so that you can quickly format the text.

continued

Several new features in Office 2007 provide tools where and when you need them. Galleries are sets of design options you can preview before applying; contextual tabs appear to offer tools for special types of content such as pictures when you select such content. View buttons make it easy to change from view to view, and a Zoom tool on the status bar makes zooming in or out quick and easy.

Gallery

Other tools offer preview galleries of effects you can apply, such as Themes or Color Schemes.

Contextual Tab

When you insert and select an object such as a table or diagram, the appropriate tools for that object appear in a tab on the Ribbon.

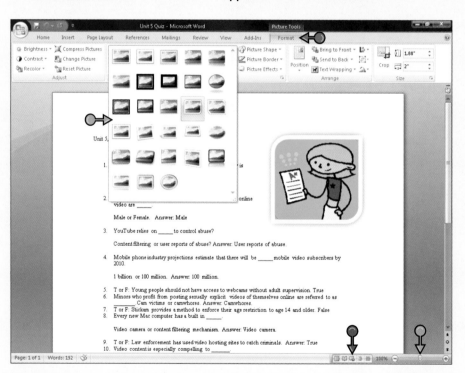

View Buttons

Click these buttons to quickly switch between views in some Office programs.

Zoom

A new Zoom tool offers an easy-to-use slider that is always available to zoom in or out.

Dialog boxes appear when there are several settings that
you may want to make at one time, such as formatting
fonts or setting print options. There are various methods
of entering or selecting options in dialog boxes.

Tab

Tabs in a dialog box contain
different sets of options in logical
groupings. Click a tab to display it.

Option Button

An option button is a small
circle. When filled (◉), it
indicates an option is
selected; when empty (○),
the option is not selected.
You can only select one
option in a group at any time.

Drop-Down List

A drop-down list box only
shows the currently selected
item in a list. Click the arrow
to open the drop-down list
and make another selection.

Spin Box

You can use the up and down
arrows on a spin box to set a
value; click the up arrow to
increase the value and the
down arrow to decrease it.

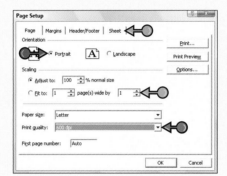

Check Box

Click a check box to toggle a
feature on and off. When you
turn a feature on, the check
box changes from ☐ to ☑.
When you turn a feature off,
the check box changes from
☑ to ☐.

List Box

A list box displays a list of
options. Click the item you
want to select. Scroll bars
allow you to move through a
longer list to see all available
options.

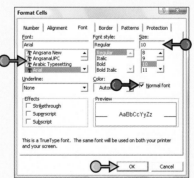

Text Box

You can enter text in a text
box; for example, you might
enter a page range to print in
the Print dialog box.

Command Button

Click a command button to initiate the command described
on the button label; for example, you can click **Cancel** to
close a dialog box without applying your settings, or click **OK**
to accept all settings you have made in the dialog box.

Using Dialog Box Controls

You can use dialog boxes to control how a feature of your program works. Dialog boxes appear when you choose certain commands on menus and toolbars.

In Microsoft Office 2007 programs, you click dialog box launchers on the Ribbon to display dialog boxes with settings related to a particular Ribbon group.

Using Dialog Box Controls

TYPE IN A TEXT BOX

① Click in the text box.

A blinking vertical line, called a *cursor*, appears inside the box.

② Press `Backspace` or `Delete`.

Any existing text is deleted.

③ Type the new text.

ENTER A VALUE IN A SPIN BOX

① Click the top arrow (⬚).

The value increases.

② Click the bottom arrow (⬚).

The value decreases.

You can also type a value in the text box next to the spinner arrows.

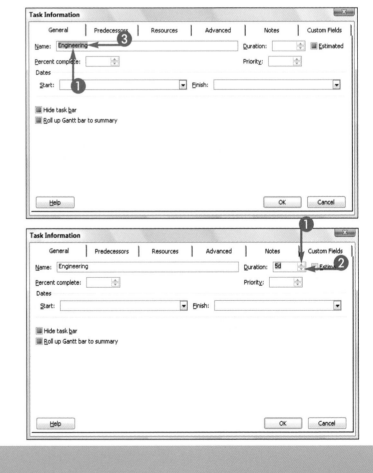

SELECT A LIST BOX OPTION

1 Click ☐ to scroll down the list.

2 Click ☐ to scroll back up the list.

3 Click an item.

The item is selected.

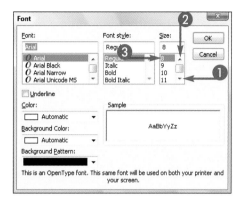

SELECT AN OPTION FROM A DROP-DOWN LIST BOX

1 Click ☐.

The drop-down list appears.

2 Click an item.

The item is selected.

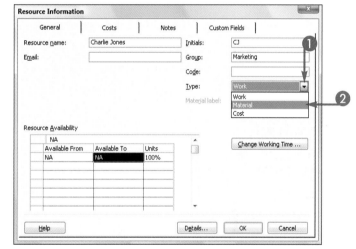

 TIPS

I cannot figure out what effect a certain feature in a dialog box will have. How can I find out more about it?

Most dialog boxes contain a shortcut to relevant help topics. Look for a Help button, or a button with a symbol such as a question mark on it, and click it to display a help window.

Some options in dialog boxes are gray and not available. Why?

In some cases you have to make one selection for those other options to become available. For example, if you do not select an underlining style in a Font dialog box the underline color option will not be available to you. In other cases you may not have hardware to support an option. For example in making show settings in PowerPoint if you do not have two monitors connected to your laptop, the multiple monitor settings will not be available to you.

Save a Document with a Different Name

You can save a file with a different name, which saves a copy of it. Any changes that you make to the copy do not affect the original document.

① Click **File**.

② Click **Save As**.

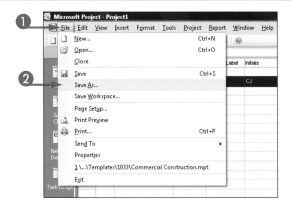

The Save As dialog box appears.

③ Click to find the folder to which you want to save the file.

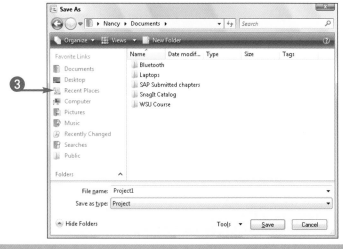

④ Click and type the filename.

⑤ Click **Save**.

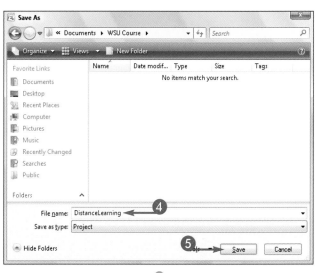

● The new filename appears in the title bar.

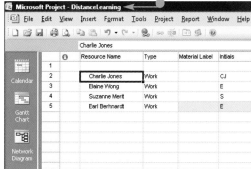

Can I make a copy of a document without opening the program in which it was created?

Yes. You can locate the document file with Windows Explorer (right-click the Windows **Start** button and click **Explore**). Right-click the file and click **Copy**. Go to a different location (you cannot save two files with the same name in one folder), right-click, and click **Paste**. You can then rename the file, if you like (this procedure is covered in Chapter 7).

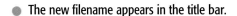

I copied a folder and tried to paste it into a folder but Windows said there was already a file of that name. What do I do?

You cannot save two files with the same name in a single folder. You could save the second file in a different folder, but it is not a good idea to have two files with the same name even in separate folders because you may accidentally overwrite a file if you save the file in the wrong folder. You could also rename the first file and then paste the second file in the same folder.

Print a Document

To obtain a hard copy of your document to give to someone else or keep in your files, you can print it.

Before you print, you must connect your computer to a printer or establish a wireless connection to it.

① Turn on the printer.

② Open the document.

③ Click **File**.

● In Office 2007 programs, click the **Office** button ().

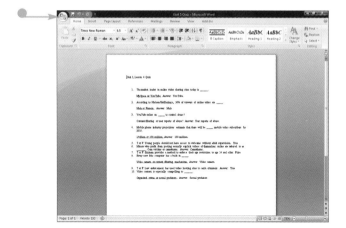

④ Click **Print**.

The Print dialog box appears.

Note: The options shown may vary by program; the Office 2007 version is shown here.

5 Type in the number of copies.

6 Click to select the pages you want to print (⊙ changes to ⦿).

In this example, pages 1 and 2 are being printed.

7 Click **OK.**

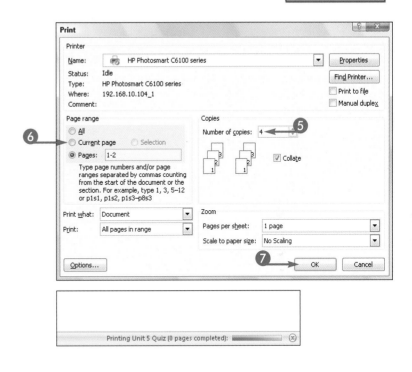

A print confirmation appears in the document's status bar while printing is in progress.

Printing Unit 5 Quiz (0 pages completed):

I want to print to a different printer than the default printer. How can I do that?

In the Print dialog box, you can use the drop-down arrow on the printer Name field to choose a different printer for this one operation. See Chapter 2 for more about connecting to a default printer.

I see an option to print to a fax. What does that do?

You can print to a fax, which allows you to use a fax software program such as Windows Fax and Scan to create a cover note and send your document as a fax via your phone line.

Uninstall a Program

If you no longer need a program, you can uninstall it to free up space for other items on your computer.

Uninstall a Program

① Click **Start** (🔵).

② Click **Control Panel**.

The Control Panel window appears.

③ Click **Uninstall a program.**

④ Click a program.

⑤ Click **Uninstall**.

In some cases, a dialog box appears, offering you a choice between making changes and uninstalling the program.

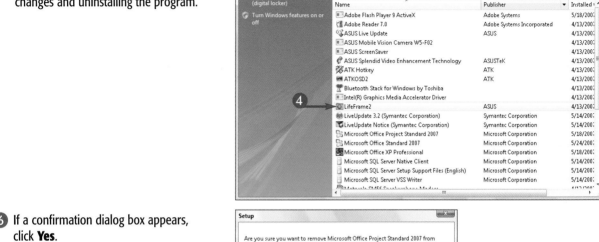

⑥ If a confirmation dialog box appears, click **Yes**.

Windows uninstalls the program.

TIP

I uninstalled a program but I now want to reinstall it. However, I get a message that I have installed the software too many times. What can I do?

Most software products allow you to install the product on two computers. When you try to register an additional copy, even if you are reinstalling it on a computer that you had installed it on previously, you may get this message. Call the company's customer support line, explain what you are doing and that you still have the product installed on no more than the allowed number of computers. They will probably provide you with a product key to complete the installation.

Using Software

Using Software 101

- Create Word Processor Documents
- Work with Numbers in a Spreadsheet
- Build Presentations
- And more...

Software applications allow you to view and play with images, listen to sound files, create and design text documents and more. Different program types are used for different reasons. For example, to write a report, you would use a word processing application; to manipulate numbers, you would open a spreadsheet application. Although applications produced by different manufacturers provide their own sets of tools and features, each category of software has several things in common. This chapter covers several of those features that many software programs share.

Create Word Processing Documents

You can create documents with a word processing application, by entering and formatting text. You can even add images for visual impact, and tables to organize information.

The Windows operating system ships with a simple word processing application called WordPad, while Macintosh computers offer TextEdit. Other popular word processing applications are WordPerfect from Corel and Microsoft Word for Mac.

Change Font

You can use type design sets called fonts or typefaces to add style to your documents. Most word processing applications offer a formatting toolbar and Font dialog box where you can choose a font and apply text effects, or formats, such as bold, italic, or underlined.

Change Font Size

To make your document easier to read or to emphasize text, you can adjust the font size. Font size relates to the height of the font characters, which is measured in points. (One inch equals 72 points.) Typically you use formatting tools or the Font dialog box to change the font size.

Apply Text Effects

Text effects, such as bold, italic, underline, or strikethrough, are great for adding emphasis or to make text more attractive or readable. For example, you might apply bold or italic effects to a heading in a report. This is usually done through formatting toolbar buttons, or in the Font dialog box.

Format Paragraphs

Paragraphs of text can be aligned along the left or right side of the page, or justified to spread across columns of text. You can also add indents to the first line of a paragraph or the entire paragraph. You can modify the spacing between lines in a paragraph, as well as the spacing between paragraphs. These changes are usually made in the Paragraph dialog box.

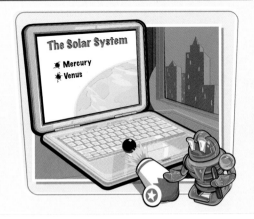

Lorem ipsum dolor sit amet, consectetur adipisicing elit, sed do eiusmod tempor inci didunt ut labore et dolore magna aliqua. Ut enim a minim veniam, quis nostrud exercitatio ullamco laboris nisi ut aliquip ex com modo consequat. Duis aute irure dolor i reprehenderit in voluptate velit ess cillum dolore eu fugiat nulla pariatur. E cepteur sint occaecat cupidatat non pro dent, sunt in culpa qui officia deserun

Add Numbering or Bullets

You can organize lists with numbering and bullet formats. Numbering is traditionally used for steps or items that follow in sequence. Bullets are used for lists of items in no particular sequence. You can apply different styles of numbering (such as Arabic numerals or outline format) and bullet symbols.

The Solar System

* Mercury
* Venus

continued

You can add visual interest to your documents with illustrations, photos, tables, or drawings. These elements can convey information in unique ways or simply make your document more attractive.

Add Images

You can add a variety of image types to your documents. For example, you might insert a photo or an illustration from a clip art collection. These images help you to make a point, or to just make your document more visually appealing.

Create Tables and Charts

Tables help to organize information into rows and columns. In word processing applications, you can change the text format, borders, and shading within the table. Charts provide data in a visual format. In some word processing applications, such as Microsoft Word, the chart program actually opens up the Microsoft Excel spreadsheet application within Word, giving you access to sophisticated charting features.

Draw

A drawing feature allows you to draw a variety of shapes, lines, and special elements such as callout balloons and banners. You click a drawing tool and then click and drag in your document to insert a drawing. You can even combine drawn objects into simple pictures.

Before you finalize your document, make sure the elements on the page fit properly and that you have used correct spelling and grammar.

Set Up Pages

A page setup feature in a word processing application allows you to perform tasks such as setting page margins, typing header and footer text for pages (such as a document title or page number), and choosing the orientation of the pages. Be sure to review the page setup settings before you print a document. The Print Preview feature in many word processors will help you see what a page will look like before you print it.

Check Spelling

You can ensure that your document is professional by running a spell check feature in your word processing application. Dictionaries are preinstalled with your program to spot misspelled words and suggest corrections. You can add words to the dictionaries and even install additional dictionaries for special words such as medical or legal terms.

Check Grammar

A grammar checker helps you to spot awkward or incomplete sentences, overuse of styles such as passive voice, and grammar errors. If grammar is not your strength, consider running a grammar check to correct your writing before you finalize your document.

Work with Numbers in a Spreadsheet

Spreadsheet programs such as Microsoft Excel and Lotus 1-2-3 provide useful tools for working with numbers and data. With a spreadsheet program, you can easily perform simple calculations and handle complex formulas.

Spreadsheets typically include individual worksheets divided into columns and rows. You enter numbers or text into individual cells.

Row

A row is a horizontal set of cells. Rows are identified by a number, with the topmost row being 1, the next one down 2, and so on.

Column

A column is a vertical set of cells. Columns are identified by a letter, with the leftmost column being A, the one to its right B, and so on.

Cell

The intersection of a row and column forms a cell. You enter data into cells.

Cell Address

Each cell in a spreadsheet has an address, which combines its column letter with its row number, such as A2 for the cell located at Column A, Row 2.

Range

You can group two or more cells into a range. The range address consists of the top-left cell and the bottom-right cell, with a colon in between. For example, B2:E6 is a cell range containing 20 cells.

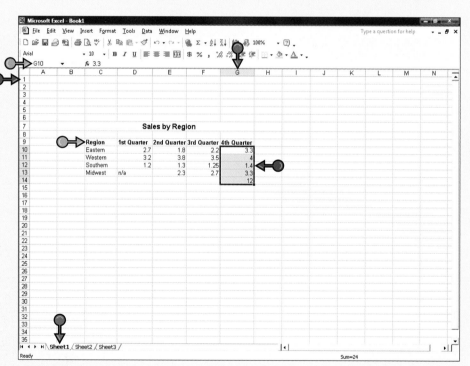

Worksheet

Spreadsheet programs typically allow you to enter work in any number of worksheets. For example, you might want a worksheet for each month of the year to enter payroll information by a particular time period. You can click a worksheet tab to display its contents.

Add Data

You can enter text, numbers, or characters into any cell. You click the cell and type the data, and the data appears in the cell and in a formula bar, which usually appears above the column headings. Press Enter to accept the entry. To edit a cell entry, click the cell again and then make changes in either the cell or the formula bar.

Add a Formula

A formula applies mathematical operations to sets of numbers or to the values in specified cell addresses or ranges. You enter a formula in a blank cell. For most spreadsheet programs, a formula starts with the equals symbol (=) and a formula such as E3-E2, which subtracts the value in cell E2 from the value in cell E3 and returns a result.

Add a Function

A function is a predefined formula that produces a calculation, such as the average of a group of numbers or a loan payment amount based on the amount, interest, and time frame of the loan. All spreadsheet programs contain a listing of predefined functions that you can use separately or within formulas.

continued

When you enter data into a spreadsheet, you can then work with that data to organize it, perform calculations, and add formatting to individual cells or ranges of cells.

Organize Data

You can use features in a spreadsheet program to sort data in a column in an order based on a criterion, such as in ascending numerical or alphabetical order. You can also filter data so that only data that meets your criteria displays, such as values over 5,000.

Calculate Values

Most spreadsheet programs provide an AutoSum feature that quickly totals the values of selected cells. An AutoSum button makes this feature quick and easy to run.

Complete a Series Quickly

If you enter a series of values or data with a logical progression, most spreadsheet programs offer a feature to quickly complete the series for you. For example, if you enter 20, 40, and 60, the program enters any subsequent numbers in increments of 20. If you enter Monday, Tuesday, and Wednesday and then drag across four other cells, the program enters the rest of the days of the week.

Format Cells

Spreadsheet programs have tools that you can use to format cells and ranges of cells. You can add shading or color to a cell, and change the font, font size, and effects. You can also modify the appearance of the border lines surrounding cells, or even remove the border lines from view.

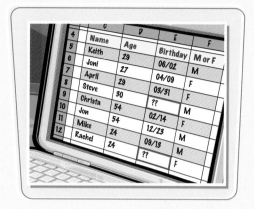

Adjust Row and Column Sizes

You may need to adjust row and column sizes to accommodate longer text or numerical values, or to insert a picture or drawing. In most programs, you move your cursor over the line between rows or columns, and then click and drag to enlarge or shrink them.

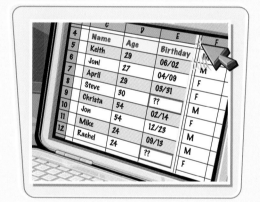

Add a Chart

Spreadsheet programs typically have useful charting capabilities. You can choose from a variety of chart types, such as bar charts and pie charts, and apply formatting to the various elements. Charts graphically represent the data that you select when you generate them.

You can use presentation programs, such as Microsoft PowerPoint or Apple Keynote, to create slides that you can use to help you communicate ideas to others. These slide shows are often used in training sessions, at conferences, or in business or sales meetings.

You can use a presentation to support a live speaker, publish it to the Web, or set it to run continuously or to be run by a viewer at a setting such as a trade-show booth or kiosk.

Slides

Slides are individual pages of content in a presentation. Each slide can contain text, images, charts, and other content items that support a single concept or idea. Bullet lists on slides are a way of summarizing key ideas to help the audience viewing the presentation to follow along.

Slide Shows

A slide show is the mode in which you run a series of slides for an audience. You can add effects that transition from slide to slide, add sounds and animation effects, and even record a narration to accompany each slide.

Add Text

Many slides in presentations include a slide title that provides the slide topic, and a bullet list of key points under that topic. You can enter text in presentation placeholders on slides, and some presentation software also offers a view where you can enter text in an outline format or with free-floating text boxes.

Add Images

A variety of visual elements can add interest to slides. You may have access to charts, tables, photos, and clip art to help you add appeal to your slides and reinforce your topic points.

Add Animations

Transition animations occur when you move from one slide to another in a presentation. A typical transition might cause a slide to appear to fly in from one side of the screen or appear in a checkerboard pattern. You can use custom animations to add motion to your slide contents, for example, by causing your bullet points to grow and shrink when you click one.

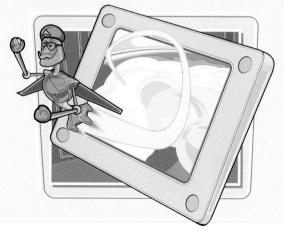

Run a Presentation

You can specify settings for how you want to navigate through your slide show. For example, you might choose to advance to the next slide either after a period of time, or manually when you click your mouse. You can also set slides to continuously loop, and run a narration for an unattended presentation.

Organize Information in a Database

A database is a collection of data that you can organize, retrieve, view, and manipulate in various ways. For example, you might use a database to store customer records or a home inventory.

Popular database programs include Microsoft Access and FileMaker Pro. Both programs are available for Windows and Macintosh computers.

Database Basics

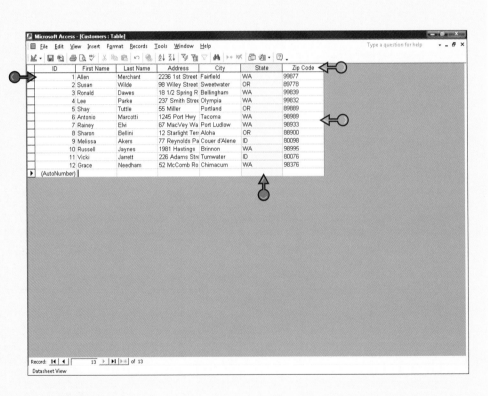

Table

A table stores a collection of related data. This might include information about your products and customers, or a collection of photos.

Field

A field is a category of data in a table. For a product table, a field might be a product model number or product name listed in a column.

Record

A record is a collection of data about one item. All of the information for one customer or product can go into a single record, typically located across a row in a database table.

Field Name

The field name appears at the top of a column of data in a database, identifying the type of data in that field.

Enter Data

You can enter data in a spreadsheet-like interface or in record forms, which you can design to look anyway you like.

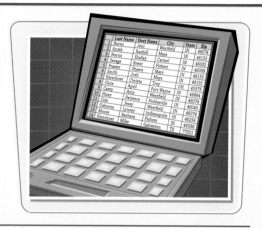

Run Queries

Queries are a way of finding information in a database that matches certain criteria. For example, you could run a query against a sales database that shows you the salespeople based in the United States who generate the highest sales.

View Reports

In database programs, you can run reports to easily view the data contained in the database. You can design the report to contain certain fields and records, and format it to make the resulting document more attractive.

Insert and Manipulate Images

You can manipulate photos, drawings, and scanned images using image-editing programs such as Adobe Photoshop or tools within presentation and word processing programs.

Windows includes a program called Paint that you can use to work with images. Mac OS X also includes iPhoto for image editing.

Digital Pictures

If you have a digital camera, you can upload your pictures to your computer using a cable that comes with your camera. Digital cameras often include software for uploading, managing, and even manipulating images.

Clip Art and Picture Files

Windows comes with a collection of photos, illustrations, sound, and movie files called *clip art.* There are also some sample pictures in your Pictures folder that you are free to use. You can download additional images from Microsoft's Web site.

Manipulate Images

By using image-editing programs or picture toolbars in other types of programs, you can resize, crop, rotate, and change the color and brightness of certain types of images.

Add Effects

Many image-editing programs allow you to retouch images. For example, you can correct the red-eye effect in photos, or add special effects by distorting an image, adding a texture to it, or tinting it to appear like an old photo.

Edit Video

There are also programs available that allow you to edit video files. Microsoft Windows includes a program called Microsoft Movie Maker, and the Apple iLife '06 suite includes iMovie HD.

Design Documents with Desktop Publishing Software

Although today's word processing programs can make your documents look great, sometimes you need a desktop publishing program to get more design features.

Microsoft Publisher, CorelDraw, and other programs allow you to use publication templates and sophisticated design tools to create greeting cards, invitations, posters, and other attractive publications.

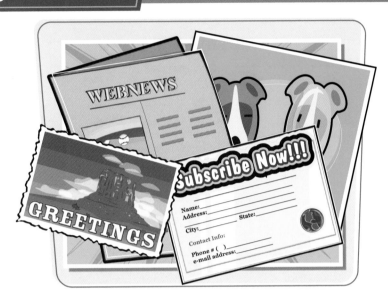

Choose a Type of Publication

Many desktop publishing applications offer a large number of predesigned templates. You begin by choosing a type of publication, such as a flyer or poster. This allows you to start from a basic design that might include some design elements and text placeholders that you can modify for your particular needs.

Design Styles

There are also sets of design options, such as color schemes, text formatting, and layouts, that you can modify in your publications. Although most desktop publishing software also allows you to build all of these elements, the publication templates and design styles can help you to save time.

Add Text

If you are using a predesigned publication template, it probably includes text placeholders that you can click in and then type text. If you do not use a template, you can draw text placeholders and place them wherever you like.

Insert Images

In addition to text, you can insert images into your publication. You can use built-in sets of design images or your own images, or you can download images from the Internet.

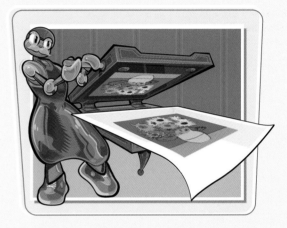

Move Objects on the Page

Desktop publishing programs allow you to modify the layouts of your pages with more flexibility than other programs. You can click and drag to rearrange text and image placeholders in relation to each other.

Arrange Text and Objects

Desktop publishing programs allow you to juxtapose text and images on a page. You can wrap text around images, and even set text to flow from one placeholder to another placeholder on a different page, as in a newsletter column.

Play Sounds and Music

Using a computer to store and play music has become a common practice. There are several programs you can use to organize and play music from a variety of sources.

Find Music

You can play music from a CD or DVD that you place in your computer drive. You can also download music from the Internet, and play music by accessing online radio stations.

Download and Share Music

Today many people are carrying small music players, such as the iPod from Apple. You can use your computer to sync with these devices to transfer music to them.

Play Music

Media players such as Mac's iTunes, and Windows-based RealPlayer and Windows Media Player allow you to organize libraries of music and play music on your computer.

Listen to Music Online

Internet radio stations allow you to tap into radio station content from around the world. You can use a media player to access these radio stations, which are typically divided into categories such as jazz, rock, and country. You can also use your browser to stream the radio station content via their Web site.

You can use your laptop to play games, which is a great way to pass the time while sitting in an airport or your doctor's waiting room.

Play Online

Many sites on the Internet enable you to play a variety of games with others. Some sites even provide virtual worlds in which you can assume an identity, known as an *avatar*, and interact with others. However, gaming sites where you interact with strangers can put you at risk if you share personal information. Always use sites that you consider reputable, and never share personal information with strangers.

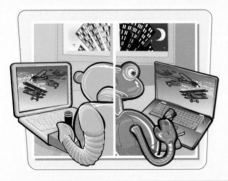

Game Programs

You can purchase games and install them on your computer, or download free games or trial versions of games from the Internet at sites such as http://games.yahoo.com.

Game Input Devices

Although most games allow you to operate them using your keyboard and mouse, some people like to attach a joystick or other type of game controller to their computer. These devices are especially popular in action games where you can use the controls to quickly zap bad guys and opponents.

Windows Vista Games

Windows offers built-in games that you can access from the All Programs folder of the Start menu. These include card games such as Solitaire and Hearts; Chess; strategy games such as Minesweeper; and even Purple Palace, which is meant for very young gamers.

Connecting to a Network

You can connect multiple computers to a network to share files and equipment, such as a printer. Today, wireless networks are available for you to set up in your home or office, or to connect to while on the road with your laptop.

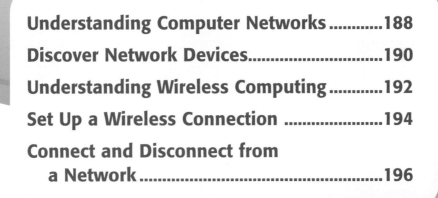

Understanding Computer Networks

A network consists of any group of connected computers. The Internet is an example of a worldwide computer network. A network connection can be set up through cables or by using a wireless connection.

Networks enable collaboration through sharing of files and equipment.

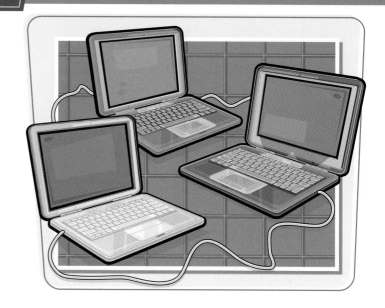

Share Files

When you network two or more computers, they can exchange files through the connection. You can control access to files by using passwords or by setting limits on the access that each network user has to folders on the network.

Share Equipment

If you have two or more computers and a single printer, scanner, or fax, everybody on the network can share that piece of equipment. You can also share hard drive space, as well as CD and DVD drives, among networked computers.

Share Internet Connections

If one computer on a network is connected to the Internet, other users on the network can access that connection. In this way, several computers can take advantage of a single account with an Internet Service Provider (ISP).

Share Storage Space

You can use one computer on a network to store copies of important files, which frees up space on other computers.

Save Money

Although you have to invest in some equipment to set up your network, this can ultimately save you money. For example, you can share equipment such as a printer, and take advantage of a single Internet connection fee for multiple computers.

Enjoy the Convenience

In a larger network, you have to spend time administering the network, while most small home networks require little administration and offer considerable convenience. Users can easily access each other's files, instead of saving files to a DVD or flash drive and walking it over to another computer to copy these files. This convenience also allows for greater collaboration between users.

There are certain pieces of hardware that you need in order to set up a network. Some hardware, such as a network interface card, is likely to be included with your computer. You have to purchase other hardware when you decide to set up your network.

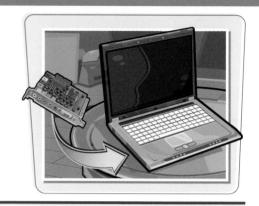

Network Interface Card

Many computers have a built-in *network interface card* – also called an NIC, network adapter, or network card. An NIC may be built into your computer in the form of a circuit board, or you can buy a PC card for your laptop that provides NIC functionality. You need some form of NIC to connect your laptop to a network.

Network Cable

If you choose to connect to a wired network, you can plug a network cable into the NIC connector on your computer, or PC card on your laptop. Data travels over the network through this cable.

Hubs

In wired networks, a *hub* provides a central connection point for every computer on the network. Data traveling between two computers on the network goes from one computer's NIC, through the cable to the hub, and then through another cable to the second computer's NIC.

Router

A *router* is a bit more sophisticated than a hub, in that it can route data to a particular network address. If you share a high-speed Internet connection, a router acts as a traffic cop, ensuring that requested data goes to the network computer that requested it.

Local and Wide Area Networks

A *local area network,* or LAN, is useful for computers that are in close proximity. You may sometimes connect your laptop to a small office or home network that is set up as a LAN. A *wide area network,* or WAN, is a collection of LANs that may be more geographically remote. These LANs are connected through fiber-optic phone lines or satellite links.

Peer-to-Peer and Client/Server Networks

Windows and Macintosh computers come with built-in *peer-to-peer* networking functionality. In this type of network, each computer handles network tasks such as file storage and resource sharing. In larger organizations, *client/server* networks are most often used. In this setup, a server handles most network tasks, and the client computers on the network are freed up to deal with end-user tasks.

Network Architecture

The *architecture* of a network establishes exactly how data is transmitted across the network. Ethernet and Fast Ethernet are popular architectures. Each type of network transmits at different speeds.

Understanding Wireless Computing

Most laptops available today have built-in wireless capabilities that allow them to connect through radio signals. In many cases, you only have to turn your computer on and let it find the nearest wireless network. Still, it can be helpful for you to understand just how a wireless network works.

Wireless Technologies

One of the most popular wireless technologies is *Wireless Fidelity,* or *WiFi.* WiFi comes in several versions, including 802.11a, b, and g, and the latest version, 802.11n. Each version has range and speed limits, with 802.11n being the fastest.

Radio Signals and Transceivers

Wireless technology uses radio signals and a radio *transceiver,* which in most cases can both transmit and receive radio signals. A wireless keyboard is an example of a device that does not have to receive data, and so it contains a transmitter that sends a signal to a receiver that you attach to your computer.

Access Points

A wireless network includes two or more computers connected through radio signals. To go online, these computers have to connect through an *access point* that establishes the Internet connection. You can set up an access point using a piece of equipment called a router to allow your computers to share an Internet connection.

Wireless Hotspots

A wireless *hotspot,* such as those you find in cafés, hotels, and airports, allows you to connect your laptop to the Internet as you roam around town or travel across the country.

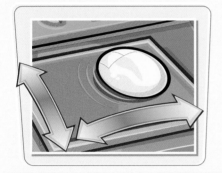

Wireless Ranges

Wireless devices have a certain range limitation. Once you move them out of range of a wireless network, access point, or hotspot, they lose their connection. If you attach wireless peripherals, such as a mouse, you can only use them within a couple of feet of your computer. In a wireless home network, you may have a range of between 75 and 150 feet, depending on the technology used by the router and your laptop.

Wireless Speeds

Transmission speeds for wireless networks are measured in megabits per second (Mbps). Using more sophisticated wireless technology such as 802.11g or 802.11n provides much faster connection speeds (as much as 100 Mbps with 802.11n), which is useful when downloading data or communicating online.

Wireless Pros and Cons

Wireless networks can offer you freedom from cords and cables. If you buy a new laptop and set up a home wireless network, the laptop is likely to recognize and connect to the network automatically. However, wireless networks can also cause your laptop to disconnect if you move too far away from them, or if there is interference from other electrical devices.

Set Up a Wireless Connection

Windows Vista provides a useful wizard to help you through the process of setting up a wireless connection.

Macintosh laptops use an AirPort card to connect to wireless networks. AirPort is equivalent to the Windows WiFi technology. Open the Network pane, choose System Preferences, and then click the Network icon to find AirPort on the Network Status screen.

Set Up a Wireless Connection

① Turn on the computers that you want to connect to the network.

② On the computer that will share an Internet connection, go online.

③ Click the **Start** button (🔵).

④ Click **Network.**

The Network window appears.

⑤ Click **Network and Sharing Center**.

The Network and Sharing Center window appears.

⑥ Click **Set up a connection or network**.

The Set Up a Connection or Network window appears.

⑦ Click one of the five options:

Connect to the Internet walks you through the steps to connect online via an Internet service provider.

Set up a wireless router or access point helps you set up a local wireless network.

Set up a dial-up connection enables you to set up a connection via a phone line.

Connect to a workplace allows you to connect via either a dial-up or virtual private network used by many corporations.

⑧ Click **Next.**

⑨ Follow the steps supplied by the wizard for the type of connection you have chosen.

Your network connection is configured.

TIPS

What do I have to do to set up a wireless access point?

When you buy the device, the manufacturer supplies specific steps for setting it up. However, you should only have to plug it into a power source, plug an Ethernet cable into it and your main computer, and turn it on.

What do I need to access a dial-up connection?

You will need a telephone cable to connect your laptop to a telephone jack, and a local access phone number. You can obtain the local access phone number from your Internet service provider.

Connect and Disconnect from a Network

You can manually connect to a network using a useful tool in the Windows taskbar. Only networks within range of your laptop are available for you to connect to.

You can also set up your laptop to automatically be detected by other computers on your network when it is connected.

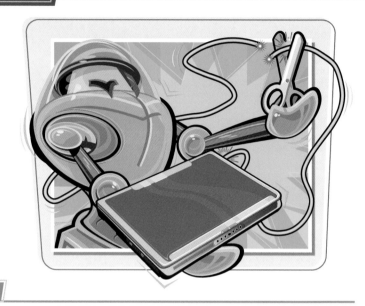

Connect and Disconnect from a Network

CONNECT TO A NETWORK

① Right-click the **Network** icon (⊞) on the Windows taskbar.

② Click **Connect to a network.**

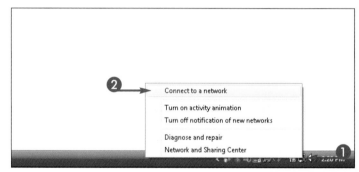

The Connect to a Network window appears.

③ Click a network.

④ Click **Connect**.

● If the signal strength is sufficient, usually showing 3 or more bars, then you should be connected to the network.

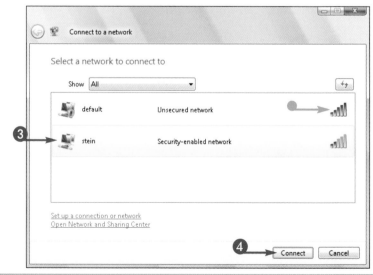

ENABLE AUTOMATIC NETWORK DISCOVERY

1 Open the Control Panel.

Note: *To open the Control Panel in Windows Vista via the Start menu, see Chapter 6.*

2 Click **View network status and tasks**.

The Network and Sharing Center window appears.

3 Click here (◉) to see more options.

4 Click **Turn on network discovery** (◯ changes to ◉).

5 Click **Apply**.

Windows applies the new setting.

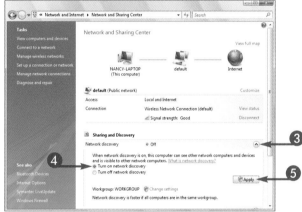

TIPS

I have connected to a wireless network. How can I share files?

The simplest way to do this is to place the files in the Shared folder on your hard drive, which you can find listed under your computer using Windows Explorer. Anybody on the network should be able to access files stored in that folder.

I see another network listed when I try to connect to my home wireless network. What is this?

It is likely that a neighbor has a wireless network and that is what you see when you list wireless networks within range of your laptop. Their security settings should keep you from accessing their network, but if not, it is not good etiquette to jump online via a neighbor's connection without their permission.

Exploring the Internet

The Internet has brought a revolution to the way we communicate, conduct business, socialize, get information, and learn. You can make use of all it has to offer with a few simple-to-learn skills.

Introduction to the Internet

The Internet is a huge global network of computers that allows people to find information, communicate with each other, access music and movies, socialize, and play games.

The Growth of the Internet

In the 1960s, a U.S. government-sponsored initiative established the infrastructure that was to become the Internet. They set up a network of computers to enable universities, research labs, and companies to work together with government agencies. In the years that followed, that network has gone beyond government use to be embraced by the public and to become global in its reach.

The World Wide Web

While the Internet is the computer network that enables online activities and interactions, the World Wide Web is essentially the system of document-sharing that resides on the Internet. This linked collection of data uses Web sites made up of Web pages where users can store and access a wide variety of data, images, and other files.

Connecting to the Internet

To connect to the Internet, you need to sign up with an Internet Service Provider, or ISP. AOL and MSN are examples of ISPs, and there are many more regional and local ISPs. You can go online using a phone line and modem (called a dial-up connection), or use higher speed technologies such as DSL and cable modems. You can also connect to the Internet through wireless hot spots, such as those in airports and hotels.

Communicating

Electronic mail, or e-mail, is a way of sending text messages, as well as attachments, to others. E-mail typically arrives at another person's Inbox a moment after you send it and, it does not cost you anything to send such a message.

Instant Messaging

You can use instant messaging services to send and receive messages instantaneously in real time. This is similar to a conversation but it takes place using text. Instant messaging is done both on desktop and laptop computers and through mobile phones and handheld devices.

Entertainment

The Internet is a wonderful place to experience media such as music files that you download to your hard drive, or online radio stations, movies, and video clips.

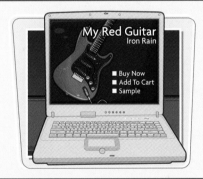

Sharing

You can share files on the Internet. File Transfer Protocol, or FTP, sites are convenient locations for document sharing. You can also use software such as Microsoft's SharePoint or hosted services to create online collaborative workspaces.

Connect to the Internet

There are some things that you need to do before you can connect to the Internet for the first time. For example, you must have certain hardware in place, and choose your Internet Service Provider.

Dial-Up Connections

Dial-up connections use a phone line to connect you to the Internet. Although higher-end, faster connection methods are quickly replacing this system, if you are on the road with your laptop and out of range of a wireless network, plugging your computer into a phone line can still work. You need a local access number from your ISP to connect to their service from that location. You cannot use the phone line for phone calls while you are connected.

DSL/Broadband

A *Digital Subscriber Line,* or DSL, also uses a phone line, but without interrupting voice service on the line. DSL is a form of broadband communication, which may use phone lines and fiber-optic cables for transmission. You have to subscribe to a broadband service and pay a monthly fee for access.

The Cost of Connecting

If you choose a phone connection, you can use your standard phone line to connect, and pay only your monthly phone bill. If you want broadband service, you must also pay a monthly subscription fee. As you travel with your laptop, you can find wireless hotspots that you can access for free in hotels, airports, cafes, and other public places. You may pay anywhere from about $10 to $50 each month to an ISP for your connection, although that cost should be part of your DSL or cable bill if you use a broadband connection.

Connection Speeds

Internet connections are delivered at various speeds. The faster the speed, the faster data can be sent, and the faster Web pages and images can display. Connection speeds used to be as low as 28.8 kilobits per second, or Kbps. Most broadband connections average around 500 to 600 Kbps. A file might take minutes to transfer over the Internet at the lower speed, and only seconds at a higher speed.

Choose a Provider

A few years ago, you signed up with a provider such as AOL, which offered dial-up access. However, today you are likely to pay a fee to access the Internet through your telephone or cable provider; companies such as AOL still offer dial-up connections, but have become mainly content providers. On your laptop, you are also likely to connect to wireless providers at hotspots in locations such as hotels and airports.

Connection Hardware

Depending on your type of connection, you will need different hardware. A broadband connection uses an Ethernet cable and modem, as well as a connection to your phone or cable line. Most laptops come with a built-in modem and wireless technology such as Bluetooth. You can also buy a wireless CardBus adapter PC card, which helps your laptop to pick up wireless signals.

Make Your Connection Secure

When you connect your computer to the Internet, other people can access your computer through that connection and cause damage to your files. To prevent this, you can turn on a firewall setting in both Windows and Mac OS.

To turn on a firewall on a Mac, click the Apple icon to go to System Preferences, click Sharing, and then use the Firewall setting to turn the feature on or off.

Make Your Connection Secure

① Click the **Start** button ().

② Click **Control Panel**.

The Control Panel window appears.

③ Click **Security**.

④ Click **Turn Windows Firewall on or off**.

In the window that appears, there will be an indication that the firewall is on or off. If it is off, proceed to Step **5**.

⑤ Click **On** (◎ changes to ◉).

⑥ Click **OK**.

Windows Firewall is turned on.

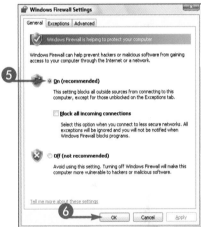

 TIPS

There is a message in the Windows Firewall dialog box that says that I am not using recommended settings. What does this mean?

In some cases, you may have another piece of software installed, such as an antivirus program, and you may also have specified that you want it to apply its own firewall. This might have overridden a Windows Firewall setting. If you want to go back to the standard settings, click the **Update Settings Now** link which appears in the Windows Firewall dialog box next to the message regarding recommended settings.

I want to use the Remote Assistance feature of Windows to have a friend help me solve a problem, but Firewall will not let me. Is there a way around this, short of turning Firewall off?

Yes, When you open the Security window of the Control Panel, click the **Allow a Program Through Windows Firewall** link. In the Windows Firewall Settings dialog box that appears, on the **Exceptions** tab, click to select the program you want to allow (in this case **Remote Assistance**), and then click **OK**.

Introduction to the World Wide Web

The Internet provides the computer network that you use to get online, but the World Wide Web provides the infrastructure for most of the information that you find online.

Web Pages

Information on the Web is delivered in Web pages. These are downloaded to your computer by a Web browser, such as Microsoft Internet Explorer and Apple's Safari. Web pages may include text, images, sounds, and even videos. There are billions of Web pages on almost every imaginable topic that are created by individuals, businesses, governments, and other organizations.

Web Sites

A collection of Web pages from a particular individual or organization is called a Web site. You may visit Web sites for a variety of reasons, such as to find information, socialize, buy or sell products, play online games, or attend a distance-learning class.

Web Servers

Web sites are stored on Web servers. These servers hold the Web pages so that people can browse through their contents. Web servers can be set up to handle heavy traffic, such as thousands of visitors, at any point in time.

Web Browsers

A Web browser is software that you install on your computer. You can use a Web browser to display Web pages. Although all operating systems include a Web browser, you can download other Web browsers, such as Mozilla Firefox and Opera.

Web Addresses

Each Web site and page has its own Web address that allows your Web browser to find it. You can enter a Web address—also called a Uniform Resource Locator, or URL—into the Address bar of your Web browser, to display the corresponding Web page, such as http://www.Microsoft.com.

URLs in Detail

A URL usually consists of four parts: the data transfer method, such as http (for Hypertext Transfer Protocol); the Web site top-level domain, such as .com for a business, .edu for a school, or .uk for a British site; the directory where the page is located (such as www.), called the third-level domain; and the domain name itself, such as Amazon or IRS. For example, a typical URL would be http://www.understandingnano.com. In many cases, you can reach the site without including the data transfer method (http/s).

Learn about Web Browsers

A Web browser is the software that you use to read documents on the World Wide Web. Web browsers also provide search capabilities.

What Web Browsers Do

A Web browser is software that you use to load and read Web pages. Web browsers typically provide tools such as a search feature, bookmarks to remember favorite pages so that you can visit them again, and a history of your browsing activity.

Windows Internet Explorer

The Web browser that comes with Microsoft Windows is Internet Explorer. You can also download the latest version of Internet Explorer from www.microsoft.com/downloads.

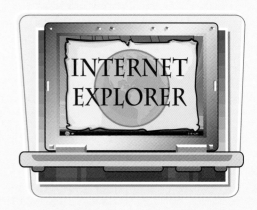

Apple's Safari Web Browser

The built-in Web browser for Mac OS is Safari. Safari is also available for use with Windows-based computers. You can download the latest version of Safari at www.apple.com/safari.

Other Web Browsers

There are several other Web browsers available, including Opera and Mozilla Firefox. Each provides its own set of features, but be aware that some Web browsers may display Web page features differently.

Navigation Buttons

Use Back and Next buttons to move from page to page. For example, if you move to a music download page, and then press Back to move back to the previous page, you can then press Next to return to the music download page. The names of these buttons might vary slightly from browser to browser.

Address Bar

All browsers offer an Address bar where you enter the URL that you want to browse. Once you arrive at a site, the actual address of that site displays in the Address bar.

Link

Browsers can take you from one Web page to another by means of hyperlinks, also called simply *links*. When you click colored, underlined text, it takes you to another page or to another location on the page. Buttons and images can also function as links.

Search Box

All Web browsers include a search feature. Enter a term in the Search box and press Enter to find Web sites and documents that are related to the search term.

Menus

Most Web browsers include menus that allow you to view favorite sites and browsing history, or to use tools to save a page's contents or send it to others through e-mail.

Search Online

You can find information or images for a specific topic by using a search engine.

You can use a search feature in your Web browser, or go to search engine sites such as Google, Yahoo, or Ask.

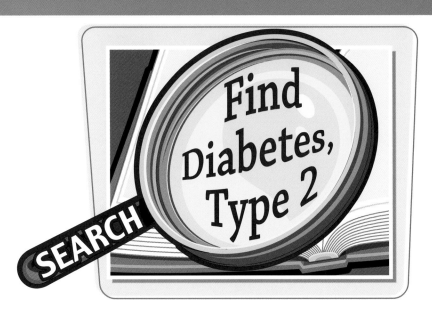

Search Engines

A search engine is a software utility that checks against a catalog of sites based on keywords that you enter. A particular site or document may have several associated keywords. Search engines return results based on a number of factors, including site ranking for popularity and relevance to the search term that you enter.

Search within Sites

In addition to searching the World Wide Web, many sites offer a search feature for finding information within their own site. They typically provide a choice to search the Web or just their site.

210

Search Types

Several search engines offer you the option of searching by types of media, such as documents, images, and sound files.

Advanced Searches

Advanced search features let you go beyond entering keywords. They might let you search for documents and sites using specified languages, file format types, domain types (such as .com or .edu), or the frequency with which your search term appears on the page.

Search Tips

To narrow down your search results, use more than one search term, such as "games, avatar, action." To search for an exact phrase, enclose it in quotation marks. You can use also certain operators with some search engines to make your search results more specific. For example, instead of entering the term "games" and getting millions of results, enter "games NOT cards" or "games AND interactive."

Using Search Results

When search results display, they are typically listed from the best match to matches that contain only a small incidence of your search term, or only one of the terms that you entered. To go to a site that is returned in a search, click the colored text link that usually appears at the top of each result.

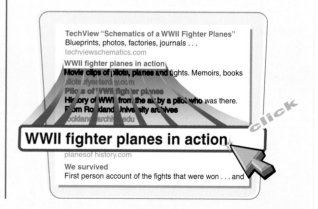

Most major network television and cable television stations, newspapers, and news magazines have Web sites that you can visit to read news stories.

You can also get current news from news blogs, news portals, or RSS syndications.

Online Publications

You can locate online versions of your favorite magazines, often referred to as *e-zines*, as well as newspapers. Some sites charge a subscription fee to access their full electronic publications; others offer at least their major stories for free, but charge for access to archived stories.

Blogs

Web logs, a term that has been shortened to blogs, may be simply a collection of personal musings by an individual, but there are also many news blogs. In fact, blogging started with journalists in war zones using the Internet to get news out when censors tried to stop them. You can find popular news blogs at www.abcnews.go.com/Technology/Blogs/ or www.nytimes.com/ref/topnews/blog-index.html.

News Portals

Sites such as http://news.google.com and www.newsisfree.com are news portals. They gather headlines from a variety of sources in one location. You can click links to see full coverage on other sites. Some of these portals have tools that let you create your own custom news page.

RSS Feeds

RSS stands for Really Simple Syndication. This program aggregates, or gathers, content that you specify and sends it to you. You can then read the content in an RSS reader. Firefox and Safari Web browsers have built-in RSS readers.

Windows Vista Feed Headlines Gadget

You can place a newsfeed gadget on the sidebar of your Windows Vista laptop. This gadget feeds top stories to your desktop. Whenever you connect to the Internet, these stories are updated. See Chapter 6 for more about using gadgets.

Research Online

The Internet is a fantastic resource for researching a wide variety of topics. You can use searches to locate information, or you can visit research sites.

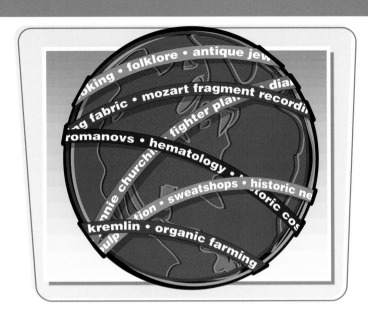

Reference Materials

Online dictionaries such as Merriam Webster (www. m-w.com) and encyclopedias such as Britannica (www.britannica.com) provide useful research information and tools. You can also find online versions of atlases, maps, and other references. Some sites, such as www.howthingswork.com and www.wikipedia.org, are constantly updated with contributions on the latest technologies and other topics.

Museums

If you are interested in topics such as art, history, architecture, science, or archeology, an online museum may be a good source of information. Visit www.coudal.com/moom to see the Museum of Online Museums. Some museums offer interactive online exhibits.

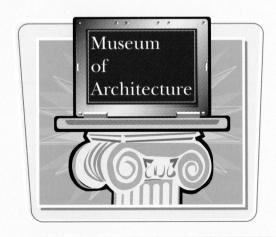

Online Libraries

Online libraries and book collections allow you to read books online, view archives of photos or videos, or download files. Visit www.libraryspot.com/libraries for a list of a wide variety of online libraries. Your local library is also likely to have an online site.

Government Sites

Government agencies at all levels maintain Web sites that offer a wealth of information. You can search for statistics; view public records such as births, deaths, and marriages; and find information about laws and topics such as trademarks and immigration.

People

If you want to find biographical information about somebody, try searching by their name, or go to sites such as www.biography.com. If you are looking for somebody's contact information online, white and yellow pages are a good resource. If it is your ancestors that interest you, then you can use a variety of online genealogy sites, such as www. genealogy.com or www.familysearch.org.

Places

Online mapping sites, such as Mapquest, allow you to locate maps and get directions from one place to another. Some locator sites, such as Google Earth at http://earth.google.com, even allow you to access satellite views of various locations.

Buy and Sell on the Internet

E-commerce is the term for buying and selling online. Web stores exist for just about any kind of product or service that you can imagine.

Online Shopping

Web stores sell a wide variety of products and services. Many provide free shipping, competitive prices, and hard-to-find items. There are online stores for popular retailers, such as Target, and for smaller specialty stores. All of these sites offer the convenience of 24-hour-a-day, 7-day-a-week shopping.

Shopping Carts

To shop online, you typically place items in a virtual shopping cart, also sometimes called a *shopping basket* or *bag*. You can view your cart at any time to review its contents, and use the cart to check out at any time. Checkout involves providing payment and shipping information. You can typically pay by credit card or with an online check payment through companies such as PayPal.

Security Issues

When you buy products or services online and provide payment information, you have to be careful to deal with reputable stores. Sites that begin with *https* instead of *http* have added security. Check the site's privacy policy to make sure that they do not sell your personal information to others. You should use a credit card rather than a debit card for online purchases, because credit cards provide fraud protection in case a site misuses your information.

Online Auctions

Sites such as eBay allow you to bid on items for sale and to place your own items up for auction. Thousands of auction sites offer specialized items such as collectibles or cars. If you buy on an auction site, you may be buying from an individual such as yourself, or a person who runs an online auction store. Using a payment service such as PayPal is a safe way to transfer money in these transactions. Always follow the auction site rules, and if others try to circumvent those rules, treat them with suspicion.

Buying from Classified Sites

Craig's List (www.craigslist.org) and other classified sites offer a virtual version of classified ads, such as those you find in your local newspaper. You can find items in your local area or around the world. Many of these sites also feature job and personal listings.

Consumer Reviews

Before you buy, either online or in a brick-and-mortar store, take advantage of online product reviews. Many online stores post customer reviews of their products directly on their product page. You can also go to consumer product review sites such as www.consumerreview.com.

Bookmark Favorite Sites

Most Web browsers allow you to bookmark your favorite sites so that you can easily return to them again.

Bookmark features can help you to organize your favorite sites. It is a good idea to periodically clear out your bookmarks so that you can easily find the ones you currently use.

Bookmark Favorite Sites

Note: *This example shows how to create bookmarks using Internet Explorer. If you are using a different Web browser, the actual steps may vary.*

① With Internet Explorer open, click **Add to Favorites** (⊞).

A drop-down menu appears.

② Click **Add to Favorites**.

The Add a Favorite dialog box appears.

③ Type a name for the favorite.

④ Click **Add**.

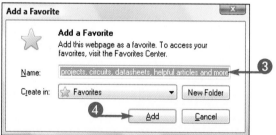

5 To display the list of bookmarked sites, click the **Favorites** button (⭐).

A pane appears listing all your Favorite sites.

6 Click the name of a favorite site.

The site displays.

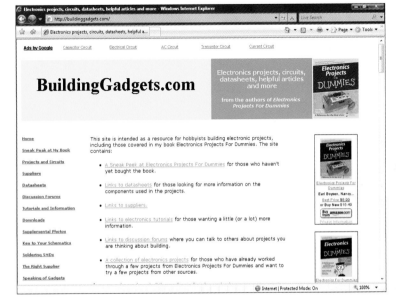

TIPS

I want to delete a site from the Internet Explorer Favorites Center. How do I do that?

Click the **Add to Favorites** button (⭐) and then choose **Organize Favorites**. In the Organize Favorites dialog box, click the item that you want to remove, and then click **Delete**.

How do I bookmark sites in Safari?

The Safari toolbar contains a button that looks like a plus sign. Click it to add a bookmark to the Bookmarks collection. You can access a bookmark from the collection by clicking the Bookmark Collection button—an open book icon—which appears on the Bookmarks bar that is located beneath the Address bar.

Communicating Online

The Internet provides many ways to communicate and connect with other people, including e-mail, instant messaging, VoIP phone calls, and social networking sites.

Understanding E-mail

E-mail has revolutionized the way that people communicate because it delivers messages and files almost instantly to others around the world.

Anybody who can access the Internet can use e-mail. You can send e-mail anytime, whereas regular mail, now referred to as *snail mail*, can only be sent and delivered at certain times. In addition, e-mail is virtually free.

How E-mail Works

E-mail stands for electronic mail. An e-mail message is sent through your Internet connection using your service provider's outgoing mail server. The message is then routed and received by the recipient's incoming mail server. The message is stored in an Inbox. The next time the recipient logs on to their mail service and checks for messages, the message is delivered.

E-mail Features

E-mail programs typically include address books for storing contact information; some design features for formatting outgoing messages; and folders for organizing and retrieving received e-mail messages. In addition, many e-mail programs provide filters to flag junk mail messages.

E-mail Accounts

You can use e-mail accounts from your ISP, or use e-mail accounts provided by other organizations such as Google or Hotmail. Some e-mail accounts are free, while others are available through your ISP for a fee. Most e-mail accounts today are Web-based, which means that you can access your account without installed software, from anywhere or any computer in the world. This ease of access is especially important to laptop owners.

E-mail Programs

You can use a variety of e-mail programs to access your e-mail. Some programs come from your ISP, while others are provided by software companies, such as Outlook from Microsoft and OSX Mail from Apple. More robust e-mail programs may provide features such as calendars, meeting schedules, sophisticated contact management, and even project management tools.

E-mail Storage

Your e-mail service provider allocates a certain amount of storage on their server for e-mail messages. You may need to pay an additional fee for more storage space. Some free e-mail services, such as Google Mail, offer as much as 2GB of storage for free. If you clean out old e-mail on a regular basis, you are not likely to ever run out of storage space.

Organizing E-mail

Most e-mail programs allow you to save incoming messages in folders. Some also provide folders where messages that you send are automatically saved, and where you can save drafts of e-mails. Other tools allow you to delete or move e-mails into other folders.

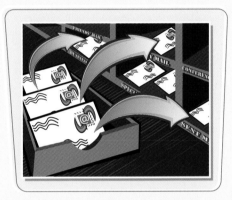

E-mail Safety

When you use e-mail, you have to be aware of certain safety issues, most of which rely on your own behavior to maintain your safety. *Spam* is e-mail that is sent out to thousands of accounts and that may contain computer viruses. In addition, *phishing* e-mails are financial scams that may encourage you to enter information such as credit card numbers or bank account numbers, which are then used to steal from you.

Discover E-mail Addresses

E-mail addresses are made up of characters that uniquely identify your e-mail server Inbox. This system ensures that a message is only delivered to the intended recipient.

Username

Your username is the first portion of your e-mail address. For example, if your e-mail address were SallyWrites@gmail.com, then SallyWrites would be your username. An e-mail service requires a unique username for every person who signs up with them. Consequently, if you try to sign up with a service and get a message that the name that you selected is taken, you must choose another unique name.

Domain Name

A domain name is located just to the right of the @ symbol in a URL; it is the name of the company that is providing your e-mail account, such as Yahoo, Gmail, or MSN. A domain name can also be your company or organization name. In the address, SallyWrite@gmail.com, gmail is the domain name.

Address Extensions

The final part of an e-mail address is the extension that identifies the type of organization sponsoring the address. For example, JoeB7@university.edu uses the .edu extension, indicating an educational entity such as a university or high school. JoeB7@university.gov indicates a government affiliation. The familiar .com and .net extensions refer to individuals or businesses.

E-mail Address Books

Your e-mail program probably includes an address book feature to help you organize your contacts. You can use this feature to address your messages to others, by selecting their address from a contact list.

Multiple E-mail Addresses

Many people today have multiple e-mail addresses. Most e-mail providers offer you several e-mail accounts, and with several providers such as Gmail offering free accounts, you can create as many accounts as you need. For example, some people use one account for their company, one for their personal use, and more for their family members. If you socialize with strangers or buy items through online auctions, it may be wise to create a separate e-mail address to protect your main account from junk mail or inappropriate contact.

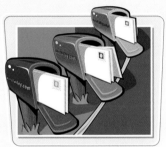

Anonymous E-mail Lists

You can create mailing lists of contacts and then hide the addressees from view when you send e-mail to the entire list. This can help to protect the privacy of individuals from others when you include them in group e-mails. Look for a group contact feature in your e-mail program to determine how to create group contacts.

Features of an E-mail Program

There are several features that most e-mail programs have in common. These features help you to send, receive, forward, and organize your messages and contacts.

Folders

Program folders are where you can store your various messages. Typical folders include your Inbox where incoming messages appear; your Outbox where outgoing messages may be held; a Sent folder containing copies of sent messages; a Drafts folder for messages that you have started but not yet sent; and a Deleted folder for messages that you have thrown out.

Inbox

Incoming messages appear in your Inbox. When you click any folder, its contents typically appear in a central area of your e-mail program.

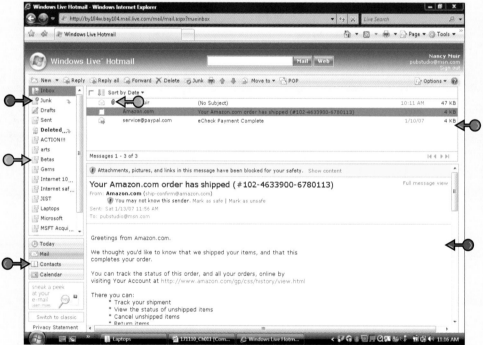

Message Preview

When you click a message, many e-mail programs display the message in a message pane.

Alerts

Next to messages in your Inbox, you often see icons that indicate when a message is urgent or when it contains an attachment.

Junk Mail Folder

Many e-mail programs contain a junk mail filter that automatically places suspicious e-mail messages in a special folder for you to review.

Contacts

Most e-mail programs contain an address book feature where you can store contact information. This makes addressing e-mail messages quicker and easier.

E-mail message forms may vary slightly from one e-mail program to another, but they have several elements in common. You will find features you can use to address a message, enter the message content, and format the content in a variety of ways.

Address fields

You can typically address an e-mail message to multiple recipients, and also use Cc and Bcc fields for additional recipients. Both send a copy to those recipients, but only the Cc field recipients' e-mail addresses will be visible to other recipients.

Subject

The subject line is usually visible in the recipient's inbox, and what you enter here will help convey your message topic and in some cases its urgency.

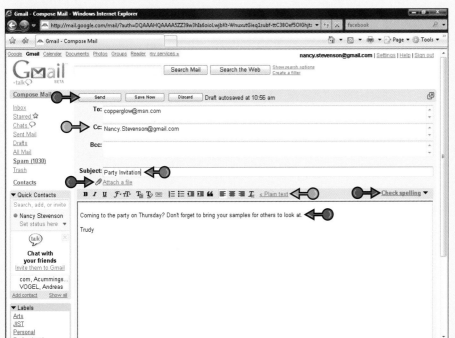

Message content

The central pane of most e-mail message forms is where you enter your message contents.

Formatting tools

Depending on your e-mail program, you will have a few simple formatting tools or a toolset comparable to some word-processing programs.

Message tools

Use these tools to save a draft, add an attachment, or send your message.

Create and Send Messages

When you know a person's e-mail address, you can send e-mail messages to that address. Messages are typically received within seconds or minutes of being sent.

If you send a message and that message is returned as undeliverable, you should check to ensure that you entered the e-mail address correctly and in its entirety.

Address Messages

Your e-mail program probably contains an address book. You can enter contact information there and then use your address book to address e-mail messages to one or more people. Some programs have a feature that allows you to begin to type an address or contact name, and the rest of the address is filled in for you. With others, you select a name from a list.

Be Brief

E-mail was never designed for lengthy communications. For one thing, it is not easy on the eyes to read long messages on a computer screen. For another, people reading e-mail may be busy, and may therefore want you to get to the point quickly. Keep your messages brief, and if you need to, attach documents with additional information.

Add Attachments

You can attach any kind of file to an e-mail, from word-processed documents to pictures and even sounds. Be careful not to attach very large items, as some e-mail services will not accept them.

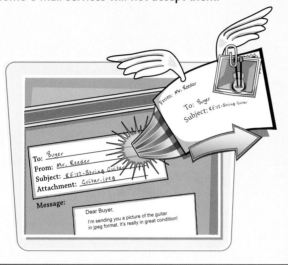

Use Smileys and Abbreviations

An entire shorthand language has been created for the Internet. Some, referred to as smileys or emoticons, use punctuation to convey feelings. For example, :-) looks like a smiling face turned on its side. You can also use abbreviations such as "lol," which stands for laughing out loud.

Proofread Messages

E-mails can be around for a long time, and be forwarded to others without you knowing it. Whether your message is a quick note or a few paragraphs, taking the time to proofread it is worthwhile to avoid the wrong tone or errors. Some people avoid typing in the recipient's e-mail address until the message has been typed and proofed, to avoid inadvertently sending off a draft before it's finalized.

Copy Others

Just as with business letters where you can send carbon copies (CC) or blind carbon copies (BCC)—left over from the days of using carbon paper to make duplicates of an original—you can send copies of e-mail messages. Use the addressing feature and your address book to add people to the CC: and BCC: fields in an e-mail message form. A CC: addressee will be visible to the main recipients, while a BCC: addressee will not.

Your ISP or e-mail company can store messages for you until you retrieve them. When you retrieve an e-mail message from somebody, there are several things you can do with it, such as read it, forward it, and reply to it.

Check Your Inbox

Depending on your e-mail program, you typically can click your Inbox folder to retrieve messages. Other programs supply a Send and Receive command or tool button. Messages are downloaded to your Inbox, unless your e-mail program flags them as junk mail, in which case they may be put into a Junk Mail folder.

Stay Secure

Incoming e-mail messages can contain dangerous viruses in attachments that can damage data on your computer hard drive, or worse. In addition, unwanted e-mail, called *spam*, can be annoying, and phishing e-mail can make phony offers that could put your financial information at risk. If you do not know the source of a message, treat it and any attachments with care. Even messages from friends can contain harmful attachments. See the next task for more about dealing with attachments.

File or Delete Messages

You can place incoming messages in folders to keep them organized. You can also create new folders for various projects and topics. It is a good practice to keep your Inbox clear of clutter. You can also delete messages that you do not need, or print a message whose contents you want to keep a record of, and delete the original.

Reply to a Message

With a message open, you can click a Reply button or link in your e-mail program to open a new e-mail form that is addressed to the person who sent you the original message. You can also use a Reply All feature to include all addressees on the original message in your reply.

Forward a Message

You can forward a message to other people who you think might be interested. When you click a Forward button or link, a new e-mail form opens containing the original message. Enter a message of your own and the recipient's e-mail address, and then send it on its way. See the task "E-mail Etiquette" for information about forwarding messages.

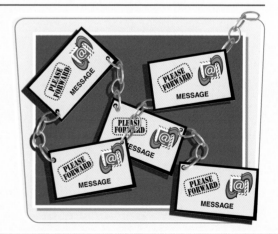

Work with Attachments

Attachments to e-mail are a great way to send information or media files to somebody else. It is important to understand how files get attached and some of the risks involved in receiving attachments with e-mail.

Understanding Attachments

Attachments are essentially electronic files that ride along with an e-mail message. Attachments can be in any file format, and created in any program. Be aware that the recipient usually needs the originating program to open the file. Some programs, such as Abode Acrobat, can read any file saved in the PDF format. Other programs, such as PowerPoint, let you embed a reader in a file so a person without that application can still view the file.

Add an Attachment

With a new e-mail message open, you can use the Attach feature to choose files to attach. If you are sending larger files, such as graphics files, you might want to save them to a compressed file to reduce the file size. See Chapter 7 for information about compressing files on a Windows Vista-based computer.

Add Multiple Attachments

You can send more than one attachment with an e-mail. The only limitation is how large an attachment your e-mail program can handle, and how large an attachment your recipient's e-mail program can handle. Keep in mind that some organizations also limit the size or type of file that their system will accept.

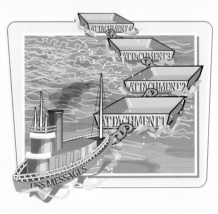

Understanding Attachment Size

Even if your recipient's e-mail program places no limitation on file size, sending a very large attachment can cause problems if the recipient has a slow Internet connection. It can take a long time to download a large file at slow speeds. If you have several large files, sometimes it makes sense to send them in a series of e-mails or post them to a file transfer protocol, or FTP, site, if one is available to you.

Open an Attachment

When you receive an e-mail with an attachment, be very careful; the attachment could be carrying a computer virus. The most dangerous type of file is an EXE file, because it carries a little program that will execute when you open it. In addition to malicious people who send you a virus, there are programs that can co-opt your friends' e-mail addresses and send out dangerous attachments using your friends' identities. Many people also forward 'cute' attachments that others send them, assuming that they are safe. Be careful—they may in fact contain viruses or a malicious executable file.

Save an Attachment

When you open an attachment, typically by double-clicking it in the e-mail message you receive, you are offered the option of saving it to your hard drive or opening it. If you save the attachment, you can choose a folder on your hard drive or storage device where you want to keep it.

E-mail Etiquette

Several rules have appeared for how to behave when writing and receiving e-mails. Known as *netiquette*, they are a continually evolving set of expected norms that those who spend time online have adopted to keep the e-mail experience a pleasant one.

Keep Messages Concise

It is not considered polite to send very lengthy e-mail messages. If you have that much to say, consider putting it in an attached document or simply picking up the phone. Also, make the subject line of your message clear so that a busy recipient can choose to read it now or put it aside for the time being, without having to read the entire message to understand what it is about.

Avoid Shouting

Entering a message in full caps is considered shouting. It conveys a feeling of anger or aggression. You can capitalize the occasional word or phrase for emphasis, but avoid full caps in most of your message.

Reference the Original Message

To help the original sender remember the topic of their message, it is helpful to either include the original message or reference it in your subject line or reply. Quoting a lengthy original message may be overkill; cutting and pasting just the most important original text may be a better option.

Get Permission to Forward

You may not intend for every communication that you send to be shared with others. Similarly, when you forward a message that has been sent to you, you should ask for the sender's permission. If there is any chance that a message's contents are private or not meant for others to see, check with the sender before forwarding it on.

Do Not Flame

A message that uses rude or insulting language is called a *flame*. Just as you do not want to receive this type of message, you should not send one. Replying to an upsetting message in the heat of the moment is not a good idea. Wait some time before replying to make sure that you do not say something that you will regret in a format that could be forwarded to others.

Be Prompt

People who use e-mail often expect it to be a fast-paced form of communication. If you use e-mail, check it regularly and get back to people promptly. Typically, you should take no longer than 24 hours to reply, and even less time if the sender has indicated some urgency.

Communicate with Instant Messaging

Instant messaging allows you to connect with people who are online at the same time as you. This is a real-time exchange of information just like a conversation, as opposed to e-mail messages for which a reply may take hours or days.

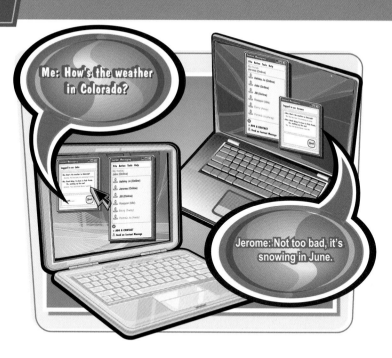

Instant Messaging Programs

You use an instant messaging, or IM, program to send and receive instant messages. Windows offers the Windows Messenger program, and Mac OS comes with iChat. You may also use messenger programs from other companies, such as AOL (www.aim.com) and Yahoo! (messenger.yahoo.com).

Your Buddy List

You can get permission from people to include them in your instant messenger program addresses, typically called a *buddy list*. Once they have been included on this list, every time they log on to the Internet, you see them listed in the IM program and you can contact them.

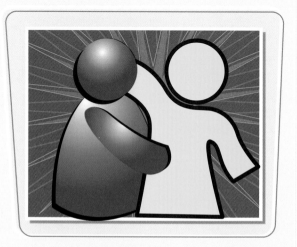

Online Status

Instant messenger programs typically allow you to set your availability status, so that those who have placed you on their buddy list can only see when you are online if you want them to. For example, you can set your status as unavailable or temporarily away from your computer. You can also block certain senders from whom you do not want to receive messages.

Send and Receive Messages

When an IM contact sends you an instant message, a window pops up where you can read the sender's message and enter and send one of your own. The messages are delivered within seconds, enabling you to carry on a text conversation.

Compatibility

Most instant messaging systems are not compatible with each other. If you have some friends who use AOL IM and others who use Windows Messenger, you will need to use both programs to stay in touch, or use an IM client such as Trillian (www .ceruleanstudios.com) which allows you to chat across multiple IM platforms.

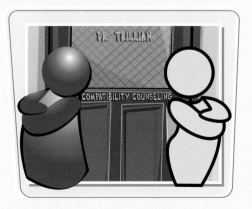

IM To Other Devices

Today, instant messages can be sent not just from computer to computer, but among a variety of devices, such as handheld computers, mobile phones, and even pagers.

Make Online Phone Calls with VoIP

You can use a technology called *Voice Over Internet Protocol,* or VoIP, to make phone calls around the world.

What Is VoIP?

VoIP is a technology that allows you to make phone calls across the Internet through electronic packets of data that contain your digitized voice. You can also use VoIP services and a Web camera, or Web cam, to exchange video images with someone during a phone call.

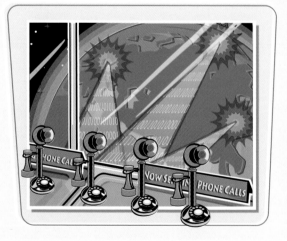

VoIP Providers

Services such as Skype and ViaTalk allow you to make calls from your computer to another computer or a traditional phone. Some VoIP companies are also coming out with pocket-sized Internet phones that work from wireless hot spots.

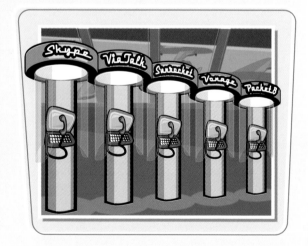

Save Money Phoning Online

You can sign up for VoIP for a subscription fee that is often much less than you would pay for a traditional phone service. In addition, there are usually no connection or per-minute charges for your calls to others on the same service, and only a small additional fee for calls to those outside of your VoIP network.

Make Phone Calls

A VoIP service is similar to e-mail in that you enter information for contacts, select a contact, and click a button to initiate a phone call. You can even set your computer up to save archived copies of your calls to play back later.

Set Up VoIP

Getting started with VoIP is simple. Once you subscribe to a service, you download a software application, plug a microphone into your computer, test for sound, and then make a test call. Typically you connect with no problem, and you can begin to call others on either their computer or phone, anywhere in the world.

Calling Features

VoIP services offer many features that you are used to on your regular phone service, including voicemail, caller ID, and call forwarding. You can also set your system up to block calls for those times when you are busy and do not want your computer to disturb you by relaying incoming calls.

Participate in Blogs and Social Sites

In recent years, the use of the Internet for social interaction has increased dramatically. Blogs are online journals where people share their ideas and thoughts. Social networking sites, such as MySpace, provide an online interactive environment.

What Is a Blog?

Blog comes from the term *Web log*. Blogs began when journalists used the Internet to record activity in war zones where censors stopped them from filing stories. Some blogs are still news-oriented, although many are simply personal journals. Blogs are interactive, meaning that the owner can post items and those visiting can respond with their own comments. Online video sites such as YouTube are a visual form of blogging where people share video clips.

What Is a Social Networking Site?

A social site is designed for social interaction. Sites such as MySpace and Facebook allow people to post personal information and interact with friends or the general public. Online dating sites are another form of social site that allow people to connect with others with similar interests for romantic relationships.

Avoid Dangers

Both social networking sites and blogs can put you at danger if you post a great deal of personal information and set your information up to be available to the general public, rather than just your friends or family. Online predators use that personal information to steal your identity, stalk you or your family, or even know when it is safe to rob your house if you reveal when you will be away from home. You can stay safer by not revealing too much personal information; not posting an identifiable photo; and avoiding settings that could expose your information to the public at large.

Create Your Own Blog

Blog services such as www.blogger.com and www.blog.com can host your blog. Most blog services charge a monthly fee, although some offer free blogs if you agree to include advertising on your site. These services also provide blog design tools and increased storage capacity for additional fees.

Sign Up on a Social Site

Social networking sites, such as MySpace.com, are typically free. You sign up by providing some personal information such as your name, e-mail address, and gender. You can also provide a photo if you want, and then make some basic settings for which visitors can view your postings and profile. A few sites, such as ASMALLWORLD, are by invitation only or are limited to people of a certain age or status, such as college students.

What to Post

You can post your ideas, your thoughts on various topics, or simply a journal about what is happening in your life. You usually create a profile that has some basic facts about you and perhaps a photo. You can also post photos and other images on blogs and social networking sites.

13

Managing Power

Laptops are first and foremost great tools for those who travel. But to use your laptop on the road, you need a charged battery or a place to plug into an electrical outlet to recharge your battery. Various settings in Windows allow you to control how your laptop uses power and how to know whether your power is running low.

Power management means understanding how your laptop uses power, and how you can get the most out of your battery.

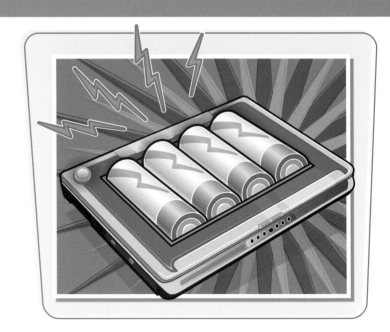

Battery Life

When you are on the road with your laptop, away from a power supply, you rely on your battery to keep your laptop working. Laptop battery life can range anywhere from one to six hours or more. By using your computer in certain ways and modifying settings, you can maximize your battery life.

What Drains Batteries Most

Obviously, leaving your computer on, or having a computer that takes longer to power down or power up, can drain your battery. A larger monitor with higher resolution or one used at a higher brightness setting can also drain a battery faster. Devices such as an Ethernet adapter or infrared transceiver can drain your battery, as well.

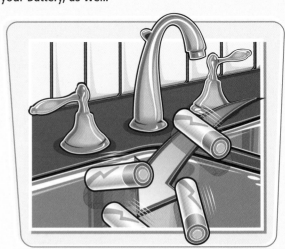

Using Adapters

When you do have access to electricity, use your adapter to power your laptop from a wall outlet and recharge the battery. Keep in mind that your laptop is likely to function only with the adapter designed for your model.

Sleep Mode

One thing you can do to help stretch your battery life is to put your laptop into sleep mode when you are not using it. Sleep mode turns off the screen and internal fan, and generally uses less energy. This mode also preserves the state of your system in RAM, meaning that when your laptop comes out of sleep mode, whatever you were doing when the laptop went into sleep mode is still open and available for you to return to work.

Monitoring the Health of Your Battery

Batteries only last so long. At some point you may notice signs that you need to get a new battery. These can include a battery that never fully charges, a battery that does not hold a charge as long as it used to, or a laptop that gets hot after running on a battery for an hour or so. You can contact your manufacturer to purchase a new battery for your model.

Choose a Power Plan

Windows Vista allows you to set a power plan (called power scheme in Windows XP) that controls how your laptop uses power.

Macintosh laptops provide an Energy Saver pane under System Preferences that you can use to make choices about power management. Use the Better Battery Life option from the Optimization drop-down list to maximize your battery life.

Choose a Power Plan

① Click **Start** (⊞).

② Click **Control Panel**.

The Control Panel window appears.

③ Click **Mobile PC**.

Windows displays the Mobile PC options.

④ Click **Power Options**.

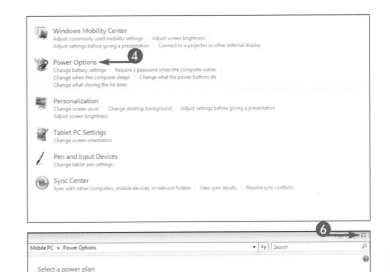

Windows displays the power options and prompts you to select a power plan.

⑤ Click a power plan to apply it (◯ changes to ◉).

Balanced provides a balance between saving power and providing higher computing performance.

Power Saver is the optimum plan for saving battery life.

High Performance will drain your battery the fastest.

⑥ Click **Close** (⊠) to close the Power Options window.

TIPS

The Power Saver plan seems good, but I would like to change how quickly the display turns off when not in use. Can I change that one setting?

Yes. You can click the **Change Plan Settings** link in the Power Options window for the plan you want to modify. In the dialog box that appears, adjust the **Turn Off the Display** setting to choose a longer time interval, and then click **Save Changes.**

I have a few more settings in my power plan than my friend has on her laptop. Why?

Some manufacturers add additional power management features to their models. This can result in there being additional settings in the Power Options window.

Adjust Screen Brightness

If your screen brightness is high, it can drain your battery power more quickly.

You can modify the screen brightness to save battery power or to make the screen easier to see in certain lighting.

Adjust Screen Brightness

① Click .

② Click **Control Panel**.

The Control Panel window appears.

③ Click **Mobile PC**.

Windows displays the Mobile PC options.

④ Click the **Adjust screen brightness** link.

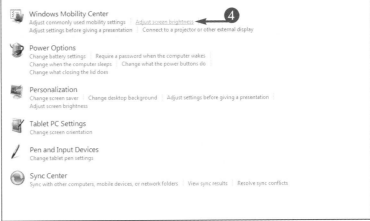

The Windows Mobility Center dialog box appears.

⑤ Click and drag the **Display Brightness** slider (🔲) to make the screen brighter or dimmer.

⑥ Click **Close** (❌) to close the window and save your settings.

The screen saver comes on when I am giving a presentation at conferences. How can I change that?

In the Mobile PC window, click the **Adjust settings before giving a presentation** link. In the Presentation Settings dialog box that appears, click the **Turn off the screen saver** check box (🔲 changes to ✅).

Why does my Mac laptop screen dim itself periodically?

Macintosh laptops have a lights-out feature that dims your screen automatically when you have been inactive for a period of time. Just start using your mouse or keyboard and the screen returns to normal brightness.

Using Batteries Efficiently

Your battery is like your computer's lifeblood when you are on the road. Knowing how to use and take care of it is vital to keeping your battery charged.

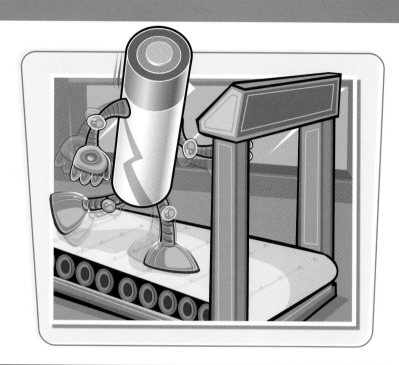

Battery Life Expectancy

Different types of batteries offer different durations for both battery charge and life expectancy. Batteries are being improved all the time, with the Lithium ion battery in most recent laptops offering the longest battery power and life. If you keep your battery for more than a couple of years, you might consider getting a new battery for your model, as all batteries eventually wear down and can hold a charge for less time than when they were new.

Develop Good Charging Habits

Getting in the habit of keeping your battery charged will save you, for example, when your cross-country flight reaches 10,000 feet and you realize you have only minutes of battery life remaining. Unless you have an older battery which requires that you wait until your battery is practically drained before you charge it, your motto should be: "Charge often!"

Determine How Much Charge You Have

Your laptop alerts you about your battery charge in a couple of ways. First, in the Windows taskbar, you can display a battery meter that shows you how much charge you have left. In addition, you can download a Windows Vista gadget that you can display in the Sidebar to reflect battery levels. You can also set a low-battery alarm to alert you when power is just about to run out.

Carry a Spare Battery

The easiest way to stretch the time you have to work on your laptop with a battery is to double your battery power by carrying a spare. The tradeoff is that you have to carry the added weight of a second battery.

Condition Your Battery

Your battery has a so-called "memory" for what constitutes a full charge. When you first purchase your laptop it is a good practice to charge it to 100 percent capacity, use the charge up completely, and then charge it again to 100 percent capacity. This is called *conditioning* your battery. Once you have done this, you no longer need to be concerned about getting the charge down to zero again before recharging.

Adjust Low Battery Notification Settings

If you are working on a vital document and your battery is low, it is helpful to receive an alert that gives you time to save your document and shut down before your computer does.

You can change the definition of what constitutes low and critical battery levels so that the notification alarm provides you with enough time to act.

Adjust Low Battery Notification Settings

① Display the Mobile PC section of the Control Panel.

Note: *To display Mobile PC options, see the section "Choose a Power Plan."*

② Click **Power Options**.

The Select a Power Plan window appears.

③ Click the **Change plan settings** link for the power plan you are using.

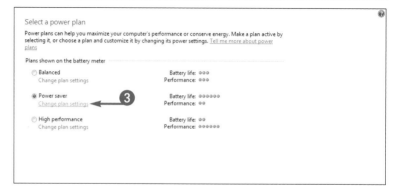

The current power plan's settings appear.

④ Click the **Change advanced power settings** link.

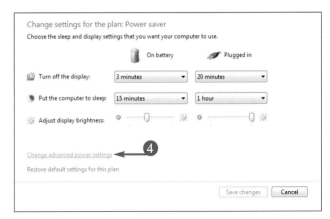

⑤ In the Power Options dialog box that appears, click the **plus sign** (⊞) next to **Battery**.

You may have to scroll down the list to locate this option.

⑥ Click either **Low battery level** or **Critical battery level** to display details.

⑦ Click the current setting and use the arrows (⬍) to modify the setting.

⑧ Repeat Step 7 for all four possible low and critical battery-level settings.

⑨ Click **OK** to apply your changes.

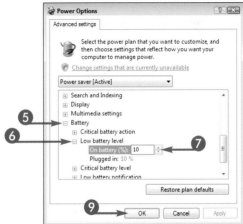

TIPS

I had the notification set for 10 minutes, but I never got a notification. Did I do something wrong?

No. It is possible that the setting for Low Battery Notification in the Power Options dialog box is turned off. Check to see if the On Battery low battery notification says Off. If it does, click the setting and choose On from the drop-down list that appears.

My laptop has slots for two batteries. Which battery is the battery meter reading reflecting?

If your laptop has two batteries, the battery meter reflects the combined remaining charge. To see each individual battery's level, hover your mouse over the battery meter and the information appears in a pop-up window.

Manage Power with Windows Vista

Windows Vista has brought several changes to the way that Windows manages power. Understanding how Vista handles power helps you to use your laptop more efficiently.

How Windows Vista Manages Power

Vista has changed the way your laptop uses power. First, it is designed for a quicker on/off procedure, so that you do not have to wait minutes for your computer to power down or power up. Second, Vista reduces energy usage if you are plugged in with a power cord.

Rapid Startup

When you push the power button on your laptop in Windows Vista you put the computer into a hibernating state. This means that your last settings and any open programs or documents are held in RAM. When you turn the computer on again, your computer returns to its previous state much faster than it would if you had to reboot it.

Rapid Shutdown

To shut your computer off Windows Vista uses a feature called Rapid Shutdown. Your computer shuts down much faster than it would if you had to power it down. This is because your system is not taking the time to give notice to applications and services that you are about to shut down and giving them each time to close. Because your current state is kept in RAM and you are not actually powering down, no damage will be done.

Let Vista Put the Laptop to Sleep

Prior to Windows Vista, you were given the option of choosing to put your computer into a sleep or standby mode, or turning it off. With Windows Vista, you can simply click the Power button at the bottom of the Start menu and let Vista put your computer to sleep. If you truly want to power down, click the arrow in the bottom right corner of the Start menu and choose Shut Down from the menu that appears.

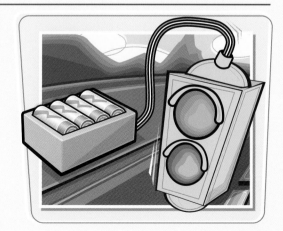

Understand the Battery Meter Appearance

With Windows Vista, your battery icon changes depending on the charge you have left. Beyond showing you the battery icon filled to a certain level, when your charge is over 25 percent, the icon will be green. When the charge reaches 25 percent, a yellow triangle and exclamation point appear over the battery icon. When the charge is extremely low, a red circle filled with a white X appears.

Maintaining Your Laptop

There are both hardware and software maintenance procedures that you can follow to keep your laptop in good condition. You can keep your operating system up to date, use Windows Vista tools to keep your hard drive running well, and perform regular maintenance on your screen and keyboard.

Update
Windows Vista

Windows is set by default to automatically download and install updates. You can change that setting in the Windows Security Center. If automatic downloading of updates is turned off, you can manually update Windows by following the steps in this task.

Update Windows Vista

① Click **Start** (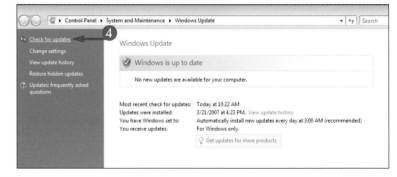).

② Click **All Programs**.

③ Click **Windows Update**.

The Windows Update window appears.

④ Click the **Check for updates** link.

Note: By default, Windows Update is set to periodically check for updates for your computer, and so you may see updates already listed in this window before you run this check.

Windows displays the Windows Update with Windows Ultimate Extras page.

⑤ Click the **View available updates** link.

A list of updates appears.

⑥ Click the updates that you want to install (☐ changes to ☑).

⑦ Click **Install**.

A progress bar indicates the download status. When the updates have been successfully installed, a message appears to let you know.

⑧ Click either **Restart Now** to reboot your computer, or the **Close** button (✕) if you would rather reboot later.

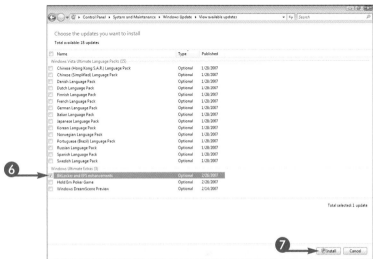

TIPS

How do I know which types of updates I should install?
Click the **Updates: Frequently Asked Questions** link in the Windows Update window to find out how updates work and which types of updates are most important.

How do I find updates for my Mac laptop?
You can do this by logging onto the Internet and clicking the Apple icon in the upper-left corner of your screen. Click **Software Updates** in the menu that appears. Mac OS checks for updates and displays a Software Update window. Use the check boxes here (☐ changes to ☑) to choose what you want to install, and then click the **Install** button.

Check Your Hard Drive for Errors

If your hard drive experiences an error, then the files that you have stored on it—including your system files—can become corrupted. When that happens, you may find that you have trouble working with programs and files. You can use a utility in your operating system, or from a vendor, to check for hard drive errors.

How Often Should You Check Your Hard Drive?

You should perform a hard drive check once a week, if possible. Windows offers a more detailed check that you can use every month to locate more obscure problems. This more detailed check can take a while to perform, depending on the size of your hard drive and the data that you have stored on it.

File System Errors

If you have ever seen a file system error message, you may have wondered what this means. Essentially, parts of your files are stored all over your hard drive. When your operating system loses track of all of the parts while trying to retrieve or save a single file, a file system error message appears.

Bad Sectors

Your computer saves data onto sectors of your hard drive. Each sector can hold a set amount of data. If one sector is damaged, your operating system cannot use the sector or retrieve data that is stored there. Checking for errors includes checking for these bad sectors.

Use Utility Software

There are software programs available that you can use to help locate and repair errors on your hard drive. Check into features of programs such as Registry Smart (www.registrysmart.com) and PConPoint (www.PConPoint.com) to see if one is right for you.

Windows Vista Utilities

In Windows Vista, you can go to your Computer in Windows Explorer and right-click a drive. Click Properties, and on the Tools tab, click Check Now. In the dialog box that appears, choose from the available options and then click Start to run the check.

Mac OS Utilities

Mac OS has an Apple Disk Utility that includes tools to repair your hard drive. This utility is located in the Utilities subfolder of the Applications folder. First select the disk to repair on the left, and then click the **First Aid** tab. Click **Verify Disk** to check for hard drive errors and Repair Disk to perform repairs.

Defragment a Hard Drive

Your operating system saves each file in small, non-contiguous sectors of your hard drive. This arrangement of file parts can eventually slow down your computer as it looks for all of the parts of each file.

You can defragment your hard drive to better organize these file parts and make it easier for your operating system to find and open files.

Defragment a Hard Drive

① Click .

② Click **Control Panel**.

The Control Panel window appears.

③ Click **System and Maintenance**.

The System and Maintenance options display.

④ Click the **Defragment your hard drive** link.

The Disk Defragmenter window appears.

⑤ Click **Defragment now**.

The process can take several minutes or longer. When defragmentation is complete, you can continue to the next step.

⑥ Click **OK**.

The Disk Defragmenter window closes with your saved settings.

 TIPS

Should I work on my computer while the disk is being defragmented?

You can work while defragmenting, but because defragmenting can take a few hours and may slow down your computer's performance slightly, you may want to run the procedure when you are not at work on your laptop.

Can I set up Windows to defragment my hard disk on a regular basis?

By default Windows performs a defragmenting routine once a week. You can modify this to occur at a different interval. In the Disk Defragmenter window click the **Modify Schedule** button and choose a different interval from the dialog box that appears.

Free Disk Space

One way to optimize your computer performance is to free up disk space by getting rid of deleted or temporary files on your hard drive. You can use the Windows Vista Disk Cleanup utility to get rid of these unneeded files.

Free Disk Space

① Click .

② Click **Control Panel**.

The Control Panel window appears.

③ Click **System and Maintenance**.

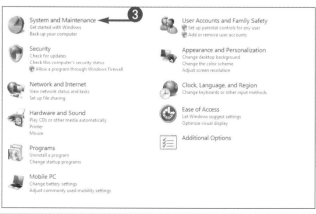

The System and Maintenance options appear.

④ Click the **Free up disk space** link.

The Disk Cleanup Options dialog box appears.

⑤ Click to select the files you want to clean up.

If you select your files, a dialog box appears, asking you to confirm which drive to defragment; choose the appropriate drive from the drop-down list and then click **OK**.

A dialog box appears, telling you how much space you can free up.

⑥ Click to select additional files to delete (□ changes to ☑).

⑦ Click **OK**.

The disk cleanup process begins; this may take a few minutes.

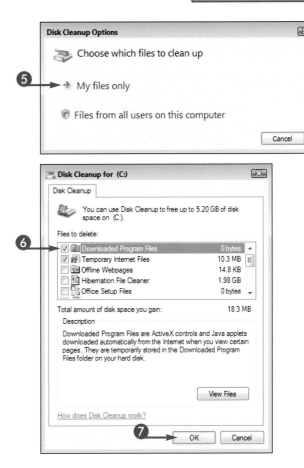

TIPS

I am a bit worried about the files that Disk Cleanup wants to delete. How can I find out more about these files?

You can easily access more details about these files. Click the **View Files** button in the Disk Cleanup dialog box to view details about the files that Windows Vista suggests deleting. These details include the size of the files, when they were created, and when you last accessed them.

Before I clean up my hard disk, is there a quick way for me to check the free space on my hard disk?

Yes. Click the **Start** menu and then click **Computer**. Click on the disk you want to check. The available space is listed there; for example, 42.1 GB free of 64.1, indicating that you have about two-thirds of your hard disk available.

Clean the Keyboard

Keyboards are somewhat open to the outside world, with spaces between the keys where crumbs and dust can get in. It is a good idea to clean your keyboard periodically to keep keys from becoming stuck or damaged.

Avoid Spills

It is a good idea to avoid eating or drinking around your laptop. Spilled crumbs of food can be cleaned out, but spilled liquids can be disastrous. If you must eat while working on your laptop, try to keep any liquids at a safe distance.

Clean the Keys

You can use a few methods to clean keys. You can buy a miniature vacuum cleaner and run it between the keys to pick up dust and crumbs that have fallen in. You can also use a non-abrasive liquid cleaner to clean the surface of the keys. Never apply the cleaner to the actual keyboard because too much of the liquid can damage it. Instead, spray a soft cloth and then wipe the keys with the cloth. Always remove the battery from your laptop before applying liquid cleaner to any part of it.

Replace a Damaged Key

You should check your owner's manual to see if your manufacturer recommends replacing damaged keys. With some laptop keyboards, you can do even more damage trying to remove keys. Others are easy to work with, allowing you to pry each key up easily (but gently!) with a screwdriver or coin. Also be aware that it is slightly more difficult to remove larger keys such as the Spacebar, because they have a metal bar across them to keep them balanced when you hit them. Again, check your manufacturer's recommendations before trying to replace a key.

Clean under the Keys

If you have a keyboard that allows you to easily remove keys, you can pry up some or all of the keys and then use an appropriate cleaner to clean underneath them.

Protect and Clean Your Screen

Laptop screens are somewhat more delicate than desktop monitors, and if you damage them, it can be costly to replace them. Take good care of your laptop screen if you want to get years of use out of it.

LCD Screens

Liquid crystal display, or LCD, screens hold a thin layer of crystals between two layers of film. Denting the film can damage crystals and therefore cause irregularities in your images, and puncturing the film can ruin your display.

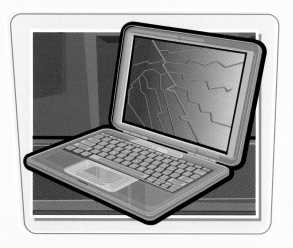

Clean the Surface Properly

Remove the battery before cleaning your screen, especially if you are using cleaning liquids. Use a special microfiber cloth (typically made of polyester and nylon) to dust the screen, and never press too hard on the screen with the cloth.

Cleaning Agents

Ammonia-based cleaning liquids, such as Windex, can damage your screen by removing anti-glare and anti-static coatings on the surface. Instead, you should use isopropyl alcohol. Do not ever spray or pour a cleaner on the monitor surface; instead, coat a cloth or Q-tip with the cleaner and rub that gently on the screen.

Protect Your Screen from Damage

When you are not using your laptop, close the clamshell lid. If you are using a tablet PC model, then buy a case for it and put it in the case when not in use. Never place sharp objects such as pens or fingernails against your screen. Extreme temperatures can also cause problems with laptop displays.

Replace a Damaged Screen

You can replace a damaged screen, although you may want to pay a professional to do it for you, because you could damage the small electronics on the side of the screen. Check your manufacturer's site for information about replacement screens, or search online to find the right replacement screen for your model.

Laptop Monitor Warranties

Many manufacturers will not guarantee laptop screens against damage; others offer protection programs that cover parts and even onsite service. Some laptop insurance policies will cover certain types of damage to your screen. Check with your manufacturer and consider whether a monitor protection plan is right for you.

CHAPTER 15

Computer Security

While most of us have learned to use our computers and the Internet in productive ways, there are some people who have taken advantage of the Internet to invade your privacy, steal your identity, and spread malicious viruses. There are several ways that you can protect yourself and your family from these threats and enjoy your time online without fear.

Understanding Computer Security

Being connected online means that you can access a great deal, but it also means that others can reach you and your computer. You can take certain steps to prevent that access and keep yourself safe.

How Intruders Reach You

Very inventive bad guys are figuring out new ways of exploiting the Internet every day. Some create viruses that are delivered through e-mail attachments, including those cute stories or animations that your closest friends forward to you, not knowing what else these attachments might do to your computer. Still others use keystroke-tracking software that you download to your computer along with shareware, to follow you around online. Some simply gather information that you have placed online on a blog or social site, to steal your identity or even sell that information to others.

Viruses

A virus is a software program created with some malicious intent, hence the term *malware*. Many viruses are sent along with e-mail, although some can be downloaded along with other files. A virus can have a range of effects, from destroying data on your hard drive to modifying your operating system. See the task, "Stay Safe from Viruses," to find out how to guard against this danger.

Spyware

Spyware attaches to other software that you download, and installs itself on your computer. Spyware can take control of your computer without your knowledge. For example, spyware might collect personal information, redirect your browser to alternate sites, or install other software.

Pop-Ups

A form of spyware called *adware* is designed to display advertising on your computer, often referred to as *pop-ups*. A site that downloads adware to your site may receive a fee for each download from advertising services. Besides being annoying, if you click a pop-up, the person controlling the site may collect your e-mail address to send spam or sell your contact information to others.

Cookies

Cookies are not necessarily harmful. Often they are downloaded to your computer so that when you return to an online store, you are greeted by name and receive purchase recommendations. Still, they are installed on your computer to help sites identify you, and many people consider this a violation of privacy. You can set up your browser to not accept cookies. Cookie manager programs such as Cookie Crusher (www.thelimitsoft.com) can also help you gain control of cookies.

Firewalls

A firewall is a software program that stops certain types of data from passing from the Internet to your laptop or desktop computer. A firewall can help to keep unwanted intruders out of your computer. Most operating systems include a firewall feature, as do many routers and wireless gateways.

Secure Site Indicators

If you submit a registration or other form online, there is a chance that the information you enter can be stolen. Look for secure site indicators, which tells you that your data is sent in a secure, encrypted form. The https prefix in a site address is an indication of a secure site.

Protect Yourself Online

One of the best ways to protect yourself online is to modify your own behavior. Just as you would not give personal information to a stranger on the street, you must learn to protect your identity and information online.

Be Careful Where You Go

You do not walk in the worst part of town at midnight. In the same way, you should only submit information or purchase items online at sites that you trust. Doing business with stores in person is one option. Another is to ask friends and associates about their experiences with an online business.

Check Credentials

You can check consumer sites, such as www.consumerreview.com, for customer comments about online businesses. You can also go to the online Better Business Bureau (www.bbb.org) to check a store's reputation. Remember, customer reviews and comments on a site are not always reliable because they may be fake.

Do Not Give Out Personal Information

If you choose to register with a site and provide personal information, make sure that the site is secure and that they do not make your information public. Many social networking and blog sites make your profile publicly available by default; you have to change the default setting to make your information private. Do not post personal information on your publicly available blog. Information about your location, your family, your income, or your activities can provide what a predator needs to locate, stalk, or rob you.

Be Careful About What Images You Post

Today many people are posting images on blogs or social networking sites. Posting images is fine, but be careful what they reveal. Is your street address or house visible in the image? Are you in a sexually suggestive pose? Is your daughter wearing a sweatshirt with her school name on it? Such images can be used to pinpoint your location, or may be modified and reposted on unsavory sites.

Do Not Fall for Scams

You have learned in your everyday life that nothing is free, and to suspect an offer that sounds too good to be true. The same is true online. Avoid store promotions that offer you the world; they are probably trying to collect your personal data to sell it or steal your identity. Immediately delete e-mails from somebody who makes unbelievable claims, for example, that you will receive a million dollars if you will only provide your bank account number for them to transfer it into. Common sense is your best friend online.

Socialize Safely

If you choose to interact with people online, whether through social networking sites, in chat sites, or in online gaming rooms, be careful what you expose about yourself. If you make a friend online, do not meet that 'friend' in person unless it is in a very public place. You should also bring another person along for protection.

Protect Your Laptop on the Road

Your laptop is especially vulnerable because of both its small size and the fact that you may take it with you to a variety of places and occasionally leave it unattended.

There are several steps you can take to protect your laptop from theft and to protect your data from prying eyes.

Fingerprint Readers

Some laptops incorporate a fingerprint reader. You can scan in your fingerprint, and then use your finger rather than a password to gain access to your system. You can also buy external fingerprint readers that perform the same function. If you are on the road with your laptop, this can be a valuable safeguard; if the computer is stolen, thieves cannot access your personal information.

Attach a Cable Lock

To prevent theft of your laptop, you may want to buy a cable lock. You can attach this cable to your laptop and lock it, and then loop the other end around an object such as a chair or your suitcase handle. This makes it less likely that a thief in an airport or hotel can simply walk away with your laptop. Check out cable locks from companies such as Targus (www.targus.com) and PC Guardian (www.pcguardian.com).

Password Protection

In the event that your laptop is stolen or accessed by somebody you do not know, your basic means of securing your information is to set a password at the operating system level. See the next task, "Understand and Use Password Protection," for more about how to do this.

Insure Your Laptop

You insure your car, so why not your laptop? Although your homeowner's insurance policy may not cover your laptop while you are on the road, you can purchase special laptop insurance that covers theft, accidental damage, or damage from a power surge. You may be able to get a rider for your home insurance policy to cover your laptop while away from home. You can also check with companies such as Safeware (www.safeware.com) to find out what their policies cover.

Use Tracking Software

FBI statistics say that one in ten laptops will be stolen in the first 12 months of ownership. You can install software such as Inspice (www.inspice.com) to help you track your lost or stolen laptop. The software can be set up to e-mail you with the location of your laptop, and allow you to remotely destroy data on it to keep people from accessing it.

Register and Engrave Your Laptop

When you purchase a laptop, you may have the option of having your name engraved on the outside. This can discourage thieves who want to resell your computer from stealing it, or help you to get it back after it has been stolen.

Understand and Use Password Protection

You can use passwords to prevent access to your computer. For example, passwords can be set on your operating system so that an intruder cannot access your system or individual files.

How Passwords Work

You can set up a file or operating system to require a password. If you or someone else cannot supply the password, then you cannot get in. This is useful to deter intruders; however, if you set a password and forget it, you will not be able to access it either. It is okay to write down your passwords, but you should never keep them near your laptop.

Picking a Safe Password

Passwords are not foolproof. Some, such as your birthdate, can be easily guessed by a person who has visited your blog or stolen your wallet. Others can be found by people using special software that runs through millions of possible combinations of words. For example, a dictionary attack uses software that runs through common words found in the dictionary in minutes.

Do Not Use Personal Information

Generally speaking, it is wise to avoid using personal information for your password. Your car model, daughter's or pet's name, or street name can be guessed by those who come into contact with you at work or in your personal life.

Use Random Characters

The safest passwords use a combination of letters, characters such as $, %, or *, and numbers. These are not vulnerable to a dictionary attack, nor can they be guessed by those who know some personal facts about you. Another trick is to use misspellings of words. A good password would be $67DtlZ*2. A bad password would be JSmith. Even though random passwords are harder to remember, the inconvenience of having your identity stolen far outweighs the effort of memorizing a safe password.

Change Your Password Frequently

You may be able to set up your operating system to require that you change your password on a regular basis, or simply remind yourself to do so. If somebody has somehow gained access to your password, changing it can protect you from future intrusions. Also, do not use the same password everywhere, such as on your laptop operating system and for your online banking or store accounts. If a thief discovers one instance of the password, they then have access to all of your accounts and data.

Disable the Guest Account

Even though you set a password on your computer, if somebody is able to log on as a guest, that person may be able to access shared files or set himself up as an Administrator with access to your other accounts. You can disable the guest account. For example, in Windows Vista, open the Control Panel, click User Accounts and Family Safety, click User Accounts, and then click Manage Accounts. Click the Guest account icon and change the setting to off.

Stay Safe from Viruses

Viruses are created with the intent of destroying or damaging your computer data. They can access your computer from a variety of sources, and you must take steps to keep your computer virus-free.

What Can Viruses Do?

A virus can damage or destroy data on your computer, make changes to your operating system settings that open up security gaps, or simply be annoying, such as a virus that makes your word-processed documents fill up with garbage text, or one that makes thousands of copies of a file until your computer memory is overwhelmed.

How Are Viruses Transmitted?

Viruses are programs. They often come attached to e-mail programs, but you can also get a virus by copying a file from a disc onto your hard drive. Some viruses are set up to co-opt your e-mail address book and send themselves out to every one of your contacts. Thinking the message is from you, they may trust it and their computers will be infected.

Be Alert to Attachments

You should learn to take care when dealing with e-mail attachments. Any file with an .exe extension at the end is an executable file, and these are most likely to contain a virus. If you are not expecting an attachment from someone, do not open it without confirming with that person that they sent it to you. Do not open an attachment that has been forwarded around the Internet, even if it comes from somebody you know. Check to be sure that your e-mail program scans for viruses before it downloads attachments. If it does not, find an e-mail program that does.

Use Antivirus Software

Antivirus software, such as Norton AntiVirus or McAfee, can be installed and set up to run regular scans for viruses and spyware. Also be sure to regularly run the update virus definitions feature, as new viruses appear all the time. Keep in mind that antivirus and anti-spyware programs use system resources, which may be a reason to buy a laptop with extra RAM and CPU-processing speed.

Read in Plain Text

In some cases, messages in the HTML format may contain scripts that are unsafe. These scripts can run when you open the message without ever downloading an attachment. If you use settings on your e-mail program to read messages in plain text instead of HTML, you will be protected from these scripts.

This is your only opportunity to cash in on the boom in real estate. Time shares are going for

Read In Plain Text

now you can make your future secure - maybe even retire a millionaire. You have until Tuesday midnight to call; after that, all offers will be withdrawn. Is this the year you

Reduce E-mail Spam

Spam is commercial e-mail that you have not requested. Spam messages typically ask you to click a link to go to a page in order to buy a product or service. Some contain offensive content; others seem harmless, but if you click a link in them, you may go to an offensive site or download spyware.

You can usually set up your e-mail program to filter spam and place it in a junk mail folder.

Never Open Spam

If you receive a message that you suspect may be spam, do not open it. Opening it can notify the sender that your e-mail account is active. The sender will then send you more spam, or sell your verified active e-mail address to others.

Never Respond to Spam

Do not send a reply to a spam message, and never click a button or link that purports to remove you from the mailing list. Any response confirms for the sender that your e-mail account is active. In fact, never click any link in an e-mail message, as that can take you to a site that contains questionable content or that downloads spyware to your computer.

Block Images and Other Content

A *Web bug* is essentially a graphic within an e-mail message that is downloaded from the sender's site when you view the image. You can set up your e-mail program to block images. For example, to do this in Outlook Express, click Tools, click Options, click the Security tab, and then click Block Images and Other External Content in HTML E-mail (☐ changes to ☑).

Anti-Spam Software

There are some anti-spam software products on the market, such as Spamkiller from McAfee (www.spamkiller.com). These programs essentially filter your mail, based on rules and lists that you set up. For example, you could set up a rule to block any e-mail with the word "sex" in the title. Many of these programs also have a feature for reporting spam and protecting you from known spammers.

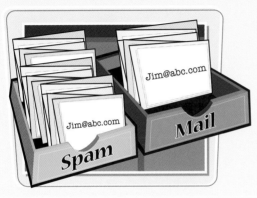

Use An Alternate Address

One way to prevent spam is to avoid giving your e-mail address to too many people or businesses. For example, when you register with a site to obtain services or make a purchase, you should set up a free e-mail account with Google or Hotmail for any confirmations to be sent to. If that account begins to receive too much spam, close it down and open a new one.

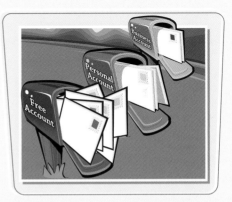

Do Not Post Your E-mail Address Online

If you participate in online discussions or post product reviews on sites, never include your regular e-mail address. People who send out spam regularly troll through those public sites to locate e-mail addresses in order to target additional victims.

Improve
E-mail Privacy

When you send and receive e-mails, you run the risk that people will access your message and use the contents inappropriately.

You can also be vulnerable to people opening up your e-mail program if you leave your laptop unattended.

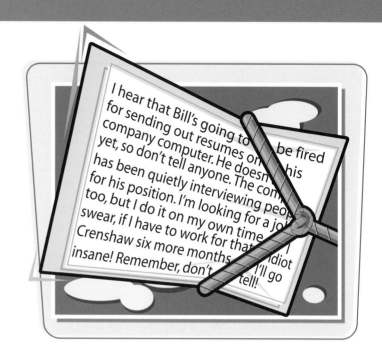

Set Passwords

Just as you can set up a password to protect access to your computer or individual files, most e-mail programs allow you to set up a password for accessing your e-mail account. See the task, "Understand and Use Password Protection," for more about creating safe passwords.

E-mail Signatures

Most e-mail programs allow you to add a signature to all of your e-mails automatically. Although this can be a convenient way to let people know your contact information when you send a message, it can also provide contact information to people who you do not want to access it. Either avoid using a signature or keep the information that it contains to a minimum. Remember, everybody that receives e-mail from you can see your e-mail address already as a way to contact you.

Public Key Encryption

When e-mail is in transit, it can be intercepted by others. To avoid this, you can encrypt messages. Encrypting a message scrambles it in a way that makes the contents unreadable by anybody. Public-key encryption buries a key value in the message, and only somebody with the key can unscramble the message.

Digital Certificates

To encrypt a message, you can use a digital ID. This certificate is given by a trusted certification authority and assures that the public key is authentic. You can include your public key in any outgoing encrypted messages that you send. Go to VeriSign (www.verisign.com) or GeoTrust (www.geotrust.com) to obtain digital ID certificates.

Encrypt Messages

To encrypt a message, you have to activate your e-mail program's encryption feature. You can encrypt messages to people who have provided you with their public key. Encrypted messages are typically indicated by a small lock-shaped icon.

Keep Kids Safe Online

You may give your children access to your laptop or even give them one of their own. If you do, be aware that children may be at special risk online, because they are not as experienced at protecting privacy as adults, and because online predators often target them.

Rather than prohibit online access and thereby shut kids off from some wonderful resources, learn how to advise and protect them about how to behave online, just as you do in the real world. A good site for advice about how to do this is Look Both Ways, located at www.look-both-ways.com.

Explain the Dangers

Children brought up with cell phones, instant messaging, and online games do not seem to recognize that they are often interacting with complete strangers, some of whom can be trusted, and some who cannot. They do, however, understand that there are dangerous people in the world, and that leaving the door to your house unlocked at night puts your entire family at risk. Get them to understand that providing their name, school name, home address (or even town), and other information (for example, when your family will be away on vacation or when they attend after-school activities) to the general public or an unknown online contact is just as dangerous as leaving your house unlocked.

Keep The Computer Public

The very best way to protect your children online is to keep the computer in a public room such as your living room. When children, including teens, are allowed to have a computer behind closed doors, you cannot control who they have contact with or what activities they engage in.

Avoid Publicly Accessible Information

If your children participate in social networking sites such as MySpace, make sure that their profiles are not publicly available, or if they are, that they do not reveal too much about the children. If you blog, do not provide too much information about yourself or your children. The information that exists about us online is cumulative, and predators can piece together a pretty complete picture of us from it if they want to.

Recognize Signs of Dangerous Activities

If your children start to receive e-mails or phone calls late at night, or if they suddenly have more money than you think they should, they may be involved in a relationship or activity online that is unhealthy. If they spend too much time in a social or gaming site, they may be developing an undesirable addiction or relationship.

Pick the Right Images

If your children post images and those images are publicly accessible, make sure that they are not personally identifiable in them, that they do not wear clothing that gives away their school or town name, and that they are not giving away personal information about your family or their friends in the images.

Filtering Software and Browsing History

You can buy filtering software that blocks your children from certain sites, based on keywords or rules that you enter. This software is not foolproof, but it can provide some peace of mind. NetNanny (www.netnanny.com) is one filtering program that is popular among parents. You can also periodically check your browser's history to see where your family members are browsing to when they use your laptop.

WEP and WPA

By using Wired Equivalent Privacy (WEP) you can protect data that you transmit across local area networks.

Understanding Wireless Standards

An organization called IEEE (Institute of Electrical and Electronics Engineers) sets standards for local area networks. IEEE 802.11 standards are used around the world for wireless connections. WEP is a security protocol defined in the 802.b standard; WPA improves on the security features of WEP and will eventually become part of the 802.11i standard.

Encryption

To send data over a wireless connection in a secure way, that data is encrypted. Encryption is a way to change data into a code that cannot be read without a key or password to decrypt it.

User Authentication

User authentication is the process of identifying a user of a network by their hardware's media access control (MAC) address. Each computer has a unique MAC address. User authentication can be used to ensure that an unknown computer cannot access the network.

WPA versus WEP

WEP is the privacy feature built into the 802.11 standard and uses encryption to protect transmitted data. WPA improves upon WEP in two important ways: by adding user authentication and improving upon WEP's encryption features.

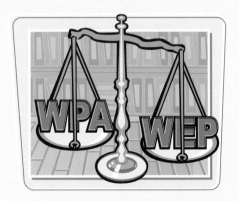

Malware is any software program that is intended to either damage or infiltrate your computer. You can take several steps to block or detect and remove malware.

Types of Malware

Malware includes several types of programs, including viruses, trojan horses, adware, and spyware. Some of these, such as viruses, can actually damage the data on your hard drive. Others such as adware are merely annoying; they may display pop-up advertisements or redirect your browser to a particular site.

How Malware Gets onto Your Laptop

Malware may come attached to an e-mail message, or may be downloaded to your computer when you click a link you find in an e-mail or on a Web site. Avoid clicking on sponsored sites that appear in search engine results and pop-up ads as these are known to put you at higher risk for malware downloads.

Blocking Malware and Spyware

There are several antispyware and antivirus software products available that you can set up to block suspicious downloads to your laptop. Turning on Windows Firewall will also provide protection against unwanted downloads.

Detecting and Removing Malware and Spyware

Antispyware and antivirus programs can also detect and remove malware from your computer. You can typically run different levels of scans using these programs. A quick scan checks the most likely locations on your hard drive; a complete or full scan checks your entire system. You can make settings to have scans run at regular intervals.

Protect Your Laptop with Windows Security Center

Windows Security Center is a central place from which you can review and modify all your security settings, including Windows Defender, Windows Firewall, your Internet Explorer security settings, and Windows Update.

Protect Your Laptop with Windows Security Center

OPEN WINDOWS SECURITY CENTER

1 Click **Start** (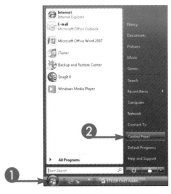).

2 Click **Control Panel**.

The Control Panel opens

3 Click **Check this computer's security status**.

The Windows Security Center window appears.

MODIFY SETTINGS

1 To view current settings for any item, click the arrow to the right of it.

2 To make settings for any of the four security features, click a link.

The associated feature opens in a window.

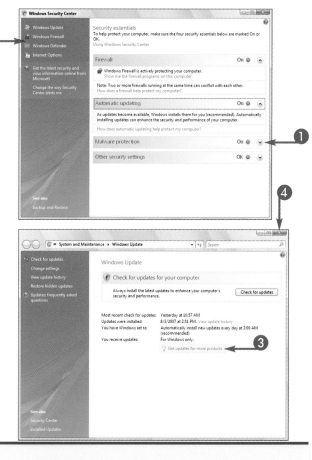

3 Use the settings in the various windows to turn a feature on or off or modify its behavior.

4 Click **Close** (![X]).

The feature window closes.

5 Click ![X].

Windows Security Center closes.

I hear that it is a good idea to have an antivirus program on my computer. Does Windows Security Center provide antivirus protection?

No. Windows offers a firewall feature and spyware protection which manages programs that track your online activities or place pop-ups in your browser, but it does not provide antivirus protection. For that, you need to purchase a third-party program such as McAfee or Norton. Antivirus programs can not only block unwanted downloads, but can also scan your system to locate and delete or isolate viruses that have reached your hard drive either from an online source or from a disc you have run on your system.

Windows recommends enabling its firewall. What exactly does a firewall do?

A firewall prevents any program from being downloaded to your computer without your knowledge. If you get a message asking if you want to download a program or allow an online site to access your computer, you are, in essence, giving permission to open the firewall up to let that program through. Be careful to whom you give such permission if you want to keep your computer safe from damaging programs or files.

Make Settings for Windows Defender

Windows Defender is a program that helps to protect your computer from malware. You can make settings to control how the various features of Windows Defender work.

Windows Defender is one of the programs you can monitor from Windows Security Center. For more information, see the section "Protect Your Laptop with Windows Security Center."

OPEN WINDOWS DEFENDER

① Click **Start** ( ).

② Click **All Programs**.

③ Click **Windows Defender**.

The Windows Defender dialog box opens.

④ Click **Tools**.

CHANGE WINDOWS DEFENDER SETTINGS

The Tools and Settings page appears.

5 Click **Options**.

The Options page appears.

6 Take any of the following actions:

● Click to turn Automatic Scanning on (changes to ✓) or off (✓ changes to).

● Click here and select either Daily or a day of the week to run a scan.

● Click here and select the time of day to run a scan.

● Click here and select the type of scan to run.

Note: You can also change the default settings for how Windows Defender responds to various levels of threat.

7 Click **Save**.

Your new settings take effect.

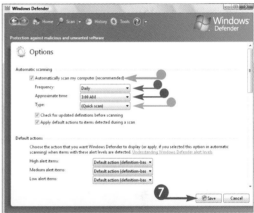

What is the SpyNet community?

Microsoft's SpyNet Community is a Web site where users of Microsoft Windows can share information about spyware programs they have encountered. Some programs that fall under the category of spyware are harmless, and may simply allow you to view your own buying history at a favorite online store. By reviewing postings on this community site you can see how other users rank programs that have not yet been ranked for risk by Windows to help you decide whether to allow them.

I have used antivirus software in the past and it required that you update definitions regularly. Do you need to do this with Windows Defender, too?

Updates are required to make Windows Defender most effective in guarding against spyware. Windows Defender works hand in hand with Windows Update, so those updates are run automatically with no effort on your part. If you are not using Windows Update, you can choose to have Windows Defender update definitions before running a scan by choosing that check box in the Windows Defender Options dialog box. The option should be selected by default.

Index

cases, 26–27
CD/DVD drives, 28
CDs (compact discs), 18
cell addresses, 172
cells, 172, 175
charts, 170, 175
check boxes, 157
chips, 54
classified sites, 217
cleaning, 269
client/server networks, 191
clip art, 180
clock speed, 21
close buttons, 152
columns, 172, 175
command buttons, 157
conditioning, 251
connectors, 24
consumer reviews, 217
contacts, 226
contextual tab, 156
Cookie Crusher, 273
cookies, 273
cooling pads, 35
corded mouse, 57
Corel WordPerfect, 143
CorelDraw, 182

D

Dashboard, 89
data
    adding, 173
    entering, 179
    organizing, 174
    retrieval, 16
    transfer cables, 24
data storage
    back up data, 18–19
    CDs, 18
    DVDs, 19

external, 28
flash drives, 19
hard drives, 14
databases, 178–179
defragmenting, 262–263
Delete folders, 226
Delete key, 71
desktop background, 110–111
desktop shortcuts, 96–97
desktops, 10
Dialog Box launcher, 155
dialog boxes
    controls, 158–159
    options, 157
dial-up connections, 195, 202
digital certificates, 285
Digital Subscriber Line (DSL)/broadband connections, 13, 202
Disk Cleanup utility, 265
displays, 51
dock
    customizing, 83
    launching items, 82
docking stations, 35
document area, 152
document design
    adding text, 183
    arranging text, 183
    design styles, 182
    inserting images, 183
    object manipulation, 183
    publication types, 182
Documents folder, 107
domain names, 224
double data rate two (DDR2), 17
Drafts folders, 226
drawing feature, 170
drop-down list boxes, 157
dual core microprocessors, 21
dual processors, 54
durability, 9

Index

Index

Index

Index

Index

Index